Quarterly Essay

For Andrew ... me

Laura

Quarterly Essay is published four times a year by Black Inc., an imprint of Schwartz Books Pty Ltd. Publisher: Morry Schwartz.

ISBN 9781760642228 ISSN 1832-0953

Subscriptions – 1 year print & digital (4 issues): $79.95 within Australia incl. GST. Outside Australia $119.95. 2 years print & digital (8 issues): $149.95 within Australia incl. GST. 1 year digital only: $49.95.

Payment may be made by Mastercard or Visa, or by cheque made out to Schwartz Books. Payment includes postage and handling.

To subscribe, fill out and post the subscription card or form inside this issue, or subscribe online:

quarterlyessay.com
subscribe@blackincbooks.com
Phone: 61 3 9486 0288

Correspondence should be addressed to:

The Editor, Quarterly Essay
Level 1, 221 Drummond Street
Carlton VIC 3053 Australia
Phone: 61 3 9486 0288 / Fax: 61 3 9011 6106
Email: quarterlyessay@blackincbooks.com

Editor: Chris Feik. Management: Elisabeth Young. Publicity: Anna Lensky. Design: Guy Mirabella. Assistant Editor: Kirstie Innes-Will. Production Coordinator: Marilyn de Castro. Typesetting: Tristan Main.

Printed in Australia by McPherson's Printing Group. The paper used to produce this book comes from wood grown in sustainable forests.

| THE HIGH ROAD | *What Australia can learn from New Zealand* |

Laura Tingle

In late March 2020, a young woman announced she was closing down her country.

"If community transmission takes off in New Zealand, the number of cases will double every five days," New Zealand's prime minister, Jacinda Ardern, told a press conference on 23 March. "If that happens unchecked, our health system will be inundated and tens of thousands of New Zealanders will die. There is no easy way to say that, but it is the reality we have seen overseas and the possibility we must face here."

Ardern had already announced a huge economic support package, including wage subsidies, on 17 March, equivalent to 4 per cent of her country's GDP. This was five days after Australia's first economic response to COVID-19, but on a scale that dwarfed the Australian response, which was around 1.2 per cent of GDP.

On 19 March, both Australia and New Zealand announced they would close their borders: New Zealand at midnight that night, Australia the day after. What triggered Ardern's move to go even further on 23 March was just two cases of COVID-19 in New Zealand due to community transmission, on top of 100 cases among travellers. Not only did Ardern close New

Zealand's borders, she shut down the domestic economy too, in some of the strictest lockdowns attempted anywhere, as shell-shocked governments around the globe tried to formulate responses to a virus that had erupted in the space of a couple of months to kill thousands and devastate the international economy. What was more, Ardern wasn't just planning to keep the virus at bay, she was planning to eliminate it. "These decisions will place the most significant restrictions on New Zealanders' movements in modern history," Ardern said. "This is not a decision taken lightly. The worst-case scenario is simply intolerable. It would represent the greatest loss of New Zealanders' lives in our history, and I will not take that chance."

She gave New Zealanders two days to get ready. At the press conference where she made these grim announcements, she was asked if she was scared. "I am not afraid, because we have a plan. We've listened to the science. We are moving early, and I just ask New Zealanders now to come with us on what will be an extraordinary period of time for everyone."

From Australia, we watched in shock, scepticism or admiration. Our political leaders were wrestling with the same issues, but prevaricating by Ardern's standards. Yes, we had moved early to close our borders to China, our largest trading partner – but closing the borders completely? And shutting down the economy?

Our path was more gradual and the messages more mixed, to say the least. On 13 March, ten days before Ardern announced New Zealand's lockdown, thousands of race fans were gathering in Melbourne for the Australian Formula One Grand Prix. The state government had so far resisted calls to cancel, and fans queued up at the gate to attend practice sessions ahead of the race on 15 March, but at the last minute the government stopped the event amid increasing alarm from public health experts about the potentially disastrous mix of local and international spectators at close quarters.

Ten days before that, on 5 March, the Morrison government had extended travel bans from China and Iran to South Korea, but argued against a ban on travellers from Italy, despite the alarming spread of the disease there.

The lead-up to the Grand Prix became a shambles, with prominent driver Lewis Hamilton highly critical of the decision to let the race proceed, and the McLaren team withdrawing after team members tested positive for coronavirus.

The economic fallout from the virus in Australia was already becoming apparent: the federal government had announced its first multi-billion-dollar plan to offset the effects. But on the day the Grand Prix was finally cancelled, things only became more confused. Prime Minister Scott Morrison announced that all "non-essential" gatherings of 500 or more people would be restricted or banned from the following Monday. But, he said, he was still planning to go the football that weekend: "I am going on Saturday because it might be the last chance for a while."

Morrison repeatedly warned that those arguing for a rapid and radical response – like the one New Zealand would soon unveil – might not like what they wished for when they got it, because opening an economy up again, once you had closed it, was difficult and complex.

In Australia we were trying to have the best of both worlds: to limit the impact of the virus, but also to limit its economic impact by minimising the shutdown.

New Zealand's response to the coronavirus is just the latest reason Australians have sometimes looked wistfully, or at least with interest, across the Tasman. Much of the recent looking has been driven by a fascination with Ardern, particularly admiration for her empathetic leadership in the wake of the Christchurch massacre, the White Island volcano eruption and the pandemic. Her stunning win in the October 2020 election gives our politicians a particular reason to look at how politics has been done in New Zealand in recent times.

But Ardern is not the first reason we have had to look across the Tasman and wonder whether there is another way of doing things. And her uncompromising positions do feel like part of a pattern. Little New Zealand – perhaps the only place in the world that has suffered isolation and the tyranny of distance more than Australia – has repeatedly jumped out of its comfort zone and changed direction harder, faster and for longer than Australia has done in the past half-century. Long before Australians noticed Ardern, its leaders were deregulating the economy more radically, cutting tax rates further, standing their ground for a more independent foreign policy against the United States and against the French over their nuclear testing in the Pacific.

When you listen to Kiwi accounts of how these things happened, there is a sort of no-nonsense pragmatism in the telling, particularly compared to the contortions of Australian politics. Consider Helen Clark on the 2003 decision not to join the Coalition of the Willing in Iraq:

> Look, you read the raw intelligence, you read the [NZ external intel-
> ligence agency] assessment. Recall the U.S. didn't give us everything.
> But it just wasn't convincing. So that was the first point, there wasn't
> the evidence. And secondly, the UN community wasn't convinced.
> It went to the Security Council, it couldn't get through. So, New
> Zealand is not in the habit of bucking decisions of the Security Coun-
> cil. That has not been our position. So, on the facts, just a no-brainer
> not to go near it.

The way New Zealanders run their politics is different too. The country has shifted from one extreme in the way it is governed to another in the past forty years: from what was sometimes described as an "elected dicta-torship" to the enforced, negotiated consensus politics of mixed-member proportional representation. From the most protected economy in the world, it has become one of the most exposed. And politicians talk differ-ently, and the political debates are conducted differently: by today's Australian standards with much more civility, for a start, and without the backdrop of the culture wars that are the stock-in-trade of Rupert Murdoch's media empire.

This essay considers some of those big political changes in New Zealand – made when Australia was confronting similar decisions – and what happened as a result. More importantly, perhaps, it considers the processes by which the decisions were made. It's not so much a recent history of New Zealand as a political and policy nerd's Cook's Tour. The idea is to offer a "sliding doors" view of a place somewhat like our own, but different, and, as a result, to afford us the opportunity to consider our decisions outside the usual box, removed from some of the inflexible boundaries which often invisibly constrain discussion in the heat of our domestic politics.

And it starts with Boris Johnson and a formidable woman with a giant spider-shaped brooch.

*

Umbria, 2019. We were sitting in the sunny piazza of a small Italian village, crouched around Glasgow George's phone, watching live as the President of the Supreme Court of the United Kingdom, Baroness Hale of Richmond (Brenda to her friends), elegantly eviscerated Boris Johnson. If her words were not compelling enough, the giant silver spider poised menacingly just below the shoulder of her court blacks was hard to ignore.

The Court had been asked to rule on the legality of the advice given to Her Majesty the Queen by newly installed prime minister Boris Johnson that the parliament should be suspended for five weeks at the height of the Brexit crisis. Even amid the turmoil of those strange times in England, the historic audacity of Johnson's advice was breathtaking. Comparable precedents raised by outraged historians went back as far as Charles I in 1629, when Britain was on the path to a civil war which ultimately didn't end well for Charles.

The unanimous decision of the court, Lady Hale announced that day in September 2019, was that any prorogation (suspension) of the parliament would be unlawful if it had "the effect of frustrating or preventing, without reasonable justification, the ability of Parliament to carry out its constitutional functions as a legislature. This court has ... concluded that the prime minister's advice to Her Majesty [to suspend parliament] was unlawful, void and of no effect. This means that the Order in Council to which it led was also unlawful, void and of no effect and should be quashed."

After all the millions of words, all the dissembling and misrepresentation of the acrid debate on Brexit, the precise legal language of the Supreme Court judges cut through with a clarity and certainty that had been missing for months. Among the Brits, Scots, Australians and Kiwis assembled in the piazza that day, cheers went up from time to time as Lady Hale coolly went about demolishing the advice Johnson had given to the Queen. It wasn't necessarily a cheer for the idea that Brexit may be thwarted. It was a cheer for governments being brought to account when they tried to pull a swifty, not just on people, but on the system.

The Brexit debate had been fought out amid a sea of bitterness, outrage and outrageous lies, and would have huge ramifications for Britain's future place in the world. But for those of us from the Antipodes, there was a piquant sense of history coming full circle: Britain's determined fight in the late 1960s and early 1970s to join what was then the Common Market had taken place in living memory. And had carried huge ramifications for us.

All around, the Umbrian countryside was a testament to what many Europeans had hoped the Common Market would help protect after the ravages of two world wars. Yet this was not the Italy where every inch of land seems to tell a tale of thousands of years of tending and cultivation. There were fields here that clearly hadn't been turned over for some time. Up on the hills, rows of grapevines had been overwhelmed by weeds and blackberries. The trees in the forest were encroaching on open fields and were themselves being choked by lantana. This part of Italy felt as though it was dying, no matter how many tourists poured in to enjoy its history. People had moved away. The small-scale agriculture of the past had become unviable.

Walking through this landscape, I recalled a visit to Brussels one freezing winter in the early 1980s, and the long corridors of the overheated Berlaymont building of the European Commission, with its smell of long-stale cigarette smoke. In those days, the relationship between Australia and Europe was one of frosty politeness rather than warmth. The United Kingdom joining what is now known as the European Union a decade earlier meant that

Australia and New Zealand no longer got the special access for their goods – their wool, meat and dairy products – into the British markets on which their economies had largely been built. It was a bit like China deciding tomorrow to trade only with, say, Southeast Asia. Except on top of the economic consequences, we were losing our sense of cultural acknowledgment, of a "specialness" in our relationship with the country from which most of us who had arrived in the previous couple of centuries had come.

In Australia in the 1970s and early '80s, hapless ministers would feature in nightly news bulletins, beating their way to London and Brussels, pledging to get better deals for our lamb and beef, our wool and dairy products. Things were even worse in New Zealand, given the dominance of agriculture in its economy. There was a profound slump. Both countries took it very personally. Having fought its wars, then fed Britain through the bleak post-war years, we had been unceremoniously dumped. To add to the pain, the Europeans were giving massive subsidies to their farmers, which made it hard for us to compete in other world markets. European "wine lakes" and "butter mountains" of overproduction, under what was known as the Common Agricultural Policy, earnt our contempt.

Ah, but what Australians needed to understand, a European Commission bureaucrat told me as he inhaled his Gauloise in the Berlaymont on that cold winter visit, was that the EU wasn't just subsidising crops to be more competitive in world markets. The Common Agricultural Policy was about preserving the European rural way of life. Free trade, he said, would kill the agricultural economies around small villages and towns that represented the soul of European societies, like the one I would be sitting in forty years later as the Brits tore themselves apart doing a volte-face. Australians and Kiwis had fought and died to protect, or rescue, those small villages and towns of Europe in World War I and II, but there was as little concern in continental Europe as there was in England, it seemed, for what it might mean for countries far away.

With the UK's Brexit decision, an apparently pointless full circle seemed to have been completed. But its trajectory was fundamental in transforming two countries at the other end of the world that suddenly found themselves out in the cold. In the wake of that original British decision, Australia and New Zealand were confronted by the need to remake themselves, or perhaps even to make themselves on their own terms for the first time – although other pressures were also building as the post-war economic order started to unravel amid inflation and new fashions in economic thought.

In the course of my research, it has been impossible not to be constantly perplexed by the strange way our two countries regard each other: all that rhetoric about ties forged in blood, and sporting competition, yet a jolly mistrust, disdain and, well, lack of interest. Until recently.

People may now remember shocks other than Britain's decision to join the EU as greater catalysts for change. But Britain played such an important part in the development of the way our two countries saw themselves in the world and – significantly – saw each other, that for my purposes it is a turning point with an import much closer to home than any other economic or geopolitical event of that period.

We have had so many hotly contested debates in Australia about change. New Zealand has confronted a lot of the same decisions, from economics to indigenous affairs, from foreign policy to welfare reform, from dealing with climate change to projecting ourselves on the world stage. The striking thing in any comparison of our respective policy and political responses is the way they start in very similar places and finish in completely different ones, having followed different paths of argument, despite much similar history and many similar institutions. Shining a light on why that is so – who and what have been influential in these decisions, and what the outcomes have been – helps reveal some of the less obvious influences shaping where Australia is now.

The fact that we have had such an obvious policy laboratory and testing ground for our own debates right on our doorstop yet know so little about New Zealand's path through this time reflects the insularity of many of the national discussions on both sides of the Tasman.

In his 2001 history of New Zealanders, *Paradise Reforged*, eminent New Zealand historian James Belich noted an "awe-inspiring" mutual neglect:

This misrepresents a shared past and also deprives historians of a rare opportunity to use each other's history as a control group, or reference point... In doing so, we not only pass up rich comparative opportunities, but also reinvent our own national histories. New Zealand and Australia, after 1901, required separateness and difference in the present, so they invented it in the past. For the nineteenth century, to an important extent, a wholly separate history of New Zealand and a separate whole history of Australia are gigantic myths, which helped make themselves true in the twentieth century.

No underlying idea has compelled the discussion forward in Australia in the past forty years so much as the idea of opening ourselves to the world. That idea inevitably raised the question of the strategic importance of our region. Yet we talk so often not in the Canberra bubble, but in the Australian bubble: as if the challenges we face are not being confronted by others. We talk of greater ties with our region, yet overlook the neighbour who is closest to us historically. It has taken a dynamic young female prime minister in Wellington to pique our recent interest in New Zealand at a time of disillusionment with our own politics. And in 2020, a catastrophic global pandemic gave us every reason not just to look at, and compare, how New Zealand was dealing with an existential crisis affecting us all, but to see our two countries in the light of a new exceptionalism.

Suddenly, the tyranny of distance which had always worked against us, and the relative success of our governments in dealing with a crisis, created a sense that we may share a potential global advantage: the Australia–New Zealand Bubble.

Britain's move into the European Economic Community, known as the Common Market, in 1973 upended Australia and New Zealand's sense of economic security. It would end the long comfort of our traditional agricultural markets: we had to find not just new markets for the goods we had always sold, but also whole new ways to make a living. Those economic changes would eventually end the overwhelming agrarian influence in politics. The old Country Party in Australia didn't just go into decline because of the drift to the cities. Policy priorities changed: in Australia, the interests of miners were pushed up the list ahead of those of farmers. In New Zealand, the National Party (always just called "National"), which had spent much of the second half of the twentieth century so far in power – boosted by its sheer geographic reach across the country on the back of agriculture's dominance – also had new battles on its hands.

Antipodean interest in the way the world worked changed. We railed against protection and special deals and became champions of free trade. There was a certain fellowship built between the two countries on our unkind treatment by the UK. And many New Zealand commentators to this day recall gratefully a sense of concern, and practical support, by Australians for their smaller neighbour in facing their mutual dilemmas: that Australia was looking out for New Zealand. Don McKinnon, who went on to become New Zealand's foreign minister, deputy prime minister and eventually secretary-general of the Commonwealth Heads of Government, recalls how Australia's trade minister, Doug Anthony, supported a Kiwi effort to secure a more preferential transitional deal than Australia's.

There were other profound global forces at work in this period, of course. The strategic world was still defined by the Cold War and the threat of nuclear war, but the Vietnam War had shaken the authority of the United States as global policeman, and Afghanistan would soon reveal the limits of Soviet power. But for a long time, we remained fixated on Britain and Europe, without seeming to notice their declining global influence.

We obsessed about their markets, instead of contemplating and exploring new ones. Our first stop when we ventured overseas as adults was London.

The post–World War II international order was starting to unravel with the end of the gold standard. There were new winds blowing through economic thought – and politics – which would see Keynesianism replaced by Milton Friedman and monetarism. That spelt a shift from confidence in the role of interventionist government to make our lives better to a disdain for its interventions and a belief in free markets – the advocacy of every man for himself: even, as Margaret Thatcher once famously asserted, the notion that "there is no such thing as society."

The OPEC oil shocks of the early 1970s provoked global double-digit inflation and unemployment, and recession. These pressures buffeted our two countries, although our political debates overwhelmingly remained framed locally. In the Antipodes, the oil shocks were felt in the form of rampant inflation and rising unemployment and attempts to beat these new forces and insulate ourselves from them. They played out in Australia in the mechanics of our local politics, already shuddering through the spasms of the Gough Whitlam era.

Australian voters had voted for change before the first oil shock, on 2 December 1972 – change not just in government, but in outlook – and were galvanised by a leader promising a more modern country, an end to Australia's involvement in Vietnam, and, at home, a new federal focus on issues that went to our quality of life, particularly in the outer suburbs. Australia was still enjoying a benign post-war world of growth, low inflation and low employment that made more government spending seem possible, if the political will and vision were there. Whitlam made university education free. There was to be universal free health care through Medibank and spending on urban development and decentralisation. Whitlam embraced culture and the arts – and, through them, a more confident sense of ourselves in the world. But the new government's agenda was thrown into disarray by the economic shock of an overnight lift in oil prices in October 1973. The new prime minister with a big social agenda faced economic issues which interested him less, and the internal chaos of a party that had been out of government for twenty-three years. The oil shocks played out as big wage claims, battles over union power, and, as the Coalition recovered from the shock of defeat, increasing attacks on government spending.

Whitlam's dismissal in 1975 provoked a new bitterness in the way politics was conducted in Australia. There were strange similarities of experience in those volatile political times across the Tasman. A Labour government had been elected in New Zealand just one week before the Whitlam government, led by Norman Kirk (whose campaign slogan, by the way, was also "It's Time"). Kirk too sought to make big changes in the way New Zealand saw itself as Britain moved away, and in its foreign policy. Like Whitlam, Kirk recognised the People's Republic of China and, in what would become a particularly significant issue later for New Zealand, his government formalised opposition to French nuclear testing in the Pacific, a move which reflected growing pressures from younger people on the left on social issues. Kirk also lowered the voting age from twenty to eighteen. The Labor government gave new status to the Treaty of Waitangi – the treaty made in 1840 between the British and a number of Māori chiefs – by making the anniversary of its signing a national public holiday and, later in its three-year term, establishing the *Treaty of Waitangi Act*, which gave legal recognition to the treaty and set up a tribunal to investigate any contemporary breaches of it.

In something of a New Zealand tradition, though, the government also sought to deal with the shocks flowing from the change in trade prospects by an extraordinary expansion of government interventions and controls in the economy. It is not being unkind to say that, in the post-war period, there was not a subsidy New Zealanders didn't like, and, even before Kirk, the country was one of the more notable welfare states among Western democracies. The new nemesis of inflation was to be confronted by fixing maximum retail prices and new subsidies for the post office, railways, milk, lamb, mutton and wool – subsidies designed to prop up jobs. There was a large boost in export and productivity incentives – and in spending on housing, education, health and welfare payments, yet also cuts in tax rates for the lower-paid. The new government even pledged a Christmas bonus – an additional week's benefit – for older people, and a new welfare payment for single parents. Not surprisingly, there was a corresponding massive increase in overseas borrowings.

The similarities between the politics of both countries in this era were even reflected in the conspiracy theories that surrounded the two ambitious governments. When Whitlam was sacked by the governor-general in 1975, there were dark suggestions that the US Central Intelligence Agency had been involved in the downfall of a democratically elected government. There were equally dark suggestions of CIA involvement in Kirk's sudden death in 1974, and in the subsequent defeat of Labour at the polls just two weeks after Whitlam was sacked.

The turmoil in Australia in 1975 had been driven by the politically relentless man who would become our next prime minister. Malcolm Fraser preached budgetary parsimony and small government in the style of Thatcher, and brought Friedman's ideas to town. The Canberra soap opera of the day swirled around federal cabinet's "razor gang" of ministers in search of budget savings, instead of the colourful lives of the old Labor ministers. Often lost in the rage of those who never accepted the legitimacy of Fraser's prime ministership – because of the way he had obtained it – was a social agenda that would be unrecognisable to the Coalition of 2020. Fraser implemented some of Whitlam's unfinished legislative plans, including on Indigenous land rights. He expanded migration, including the mass arrival of Vietnamese refugees by boat. He campaigned on the global stage against the apartheid policies of South Africa. This would eventually put him on the other side of a bitter battle fought by his Kiwi counterpart, Sir Robert Muldoon, which provoked some of the deepest schisms in recent memory in New Zealand.

"Piggy" Muldoon was an aggressive, ruthless, divisive, deeply unpleasant man who raged against the world – from the mighty to the minnows – and relentlessly exploited New Zealand's unicameral political system to centralise power in his own hands.

Australian policy debates have often been redolent with regret that we did not have the same unicameral system of government as New Zealand, which, since 1951, has had just one chamber of parliament, not a Senate or state governments. This was seen, for example, as a great hindrance to the deregulation of Australia during the reform era of the 1980s and '90s. But of course, in earlier times, it also meant New Zealand prime ministers had immense powers to control the economy which would horrify conservatives today.

Former prime minister Geoffrey Palmer, a constitutional lawyer, described Muldoon as running an elected dictatorship between 1975 and 1984, recalling that when he became deputy Labour leader to David Lange in 1983 and they ordered a couch for their office, "the request was denied – not by some bureaucrat but by Muldoon himself. The prime minister would decide the level of comfort to which his opponents would become accustomed." Muldoon's political pitch was to the "ordinary bloke" in New Zealand: a belligerent champion, particularly of older Kiwis resistant to the changes and uncertainty swirling in the world when he was elected prime minister in 1975.

South Africa's rugby union team – the Springboks – were set to tour New Zealand in 1981, amid bitter protests. The team was one of the then rogue nation's last links with a world that had made the country a pariah over apartheid. Fraser would not even let their plane land in Australia to refuel. But Muldoon – a prime minister who raised the art of governmental and prime ministerial intervention to its high point in New Zealand – declined to intervene to stop the tour, implicitly siding with the rugby supporters who backed it. It is hard to appreciate from afar what a shockwave the tour caused in what was generally a quiet and peaceful country, but its ugliness is there for all to see in footage of events at a game, subsequently called off, in Hamilton on 25 July. Anti-apartheid protesters – mostly a rather daggy collection of middle-aged academics in bad knitwear– are confronted and assaulted first by jogging walls of riot police, who physically drag many of them from the field, and then by a baying crowd angered at the cancellation of the game.

Muldoon's popularity had been in decline since his first landslide win in 1975, and when he went to the polls for a third term in that bitter year of the Springbok tour, on 28 November 1981, he won the majority of seats – a majority of one – although the opposition Labour Party won the largest share of votes.

The sense that a tipping point in New Zealand politics was not far off was pervasive. Pressure to address Māori inequality and gay rights was increasing at home. The anti-nuclear issue also continued to gather momentum, staunchly resisted by Muldoon, who told his colleagues to ignore it, arguing New Zealanders would never vote on a defence issue. However, it would be this that ultimately led to his political demise.

The social divisions in New Zealand and Australia during the late 1970s and early 1980s sometimes masked the fact that both governments of the day were writhing uncomfortably in the grip of unprecedented economic experience – simultaneous high inflation and unemployment. As their long prime ministerships started to fade, both Muldoon and Fraser would lurch around in search of signature policies to deal with these pressures and show them standing successfully against the tide of change. In New Zealand, Muldoon had "Think Big" – a series of projects of questionable value, from fuel plants to dams, funded by overseas borrowings, designed to make New Zealand more energy self-sufficient in the wake of the oil shocks and to allow the country to develop local big industry, such as alu-minium production, using relatively cheap energy, including the highly controversial Clyde Dam on the South Island.

With his popularity on the wane after the 1981 election, Muldoon announced a wage and price freeze in 1982. It covered not just wages and retail prices, but interest rates, dividends and rents. In fact, everything was regulated except the share market and the costs of Think Big projects, which escalated. Inevitably, the freeze distorted prices and, as a result, put pressure on the fixed exchange rate – leading to inexorable pressure for it to be devalued – and sowed the seeds of a share-market bubble which would have catastrophic effects later in the decade. But the NZ welfare state continued on apace. When Muldoon lost power in 1984, it was estimated that the average subsidy paid to every Kiwi farmer was $40,000 a year. Government support for agriculture had grown from just 3 per cent of farm income in the 1960s to nearly 40 per cent for sheep farmers alone, a bill equivalent to 4 per cent of GDP.

In Australia, Fraser's apparent invincibility and domination of the political landscape since the sacking of Whitlam in 1975 had also been shaken by a closer-than-expected election result, in 1980. In a reflection of Think Big, Fraser was enthused by the possibility of a massive resources boom in Australia in the wake of the second OPEC oil shock, and encouraged, even goaded, by the states to borrow big to build energy and other infrastructure to support the boom. But he had still not conquered inflation, and in 1981 he reined in budget borrowing and spending just as the economy started to fall into what would be the recession of the early 1980s. It would be wages, though, that set up an air of confrontation and failure in the lead-up to his last election. While Fraser and his government often railed against Australia's centralised wage-fixing system, they had no alternative to offer. The promised resources boom and the inflexibility of Australia's wages system came together to produce a new wages push. Wages had risen 14 per cent in the year to December 1980, and in the middle of June 1981 transport workers launched a campaign for an extra $20 a week, backed by a crippling strike. In the free-for-all that followed, the ideological divisions within the Liberal Party started to widen, and the push for deregulation of the economy increased.

It was a perfect stage for the man who would become the next prime minister to make his entrance. Bob Hawke was a master of the industrial realm, seen by the Australian public as the ultimate conciliator of disputes.

Both Muldoon and Fraser would ultimately be undone by a spectacular miscalculation in calling an election. On 3 February 1983, Fraser raced to announce a poll to head off an expected change of Labor leadership from Bill Hayden to Bob Hawke, unaware that the change of Opposition leader had occurred two hours earlier. Just over a year later, a drunk Muldoon called a snap election when confronted by a government MP threatening to cross the floor against him on the anti-nuclear issue, and lost. Both men would be defeated by charismatic leaders from labour movements weary of being in opposition, containing a new generation of politicians open to new ideas and new ways of conducting politics.

*

And this is where our story really takes off.

Hawke had won government on a platform of reconciliation, recovery and reconstruction, built on his reputation as an industrial conciliator, and promising a new cooperation after the divisive Fraser years. The centrepiece of his administration was to be an agreement between government and unions. Following the disarray of wages policy under Fraser, Labor sought to turn its relationship with the trade unions into a positive. Shadow treasurer and industrial relations minister Ralph Willis and the ACTU's Jan Marsh fashioned a Prices and Incomes Accord, which traded wage restraint for a pledge that Labor would deliver a "social wage": benefits that would improve quality of life and working conditions. There was also a promise to provide free health care – as Whitlam had attempted.

Hawke's late ascension to the leadership meant Labor went into the election campaign led by a political figure who embodied a change away from the confrontational political and industrial years. But the dramas that dominated 1983 were shaped by developments beyond Hawke's control. The global pressures that had been building for so long – inflation, recession, changing economic fashions – manifested themselves in speculation on the value of the Australian dollar, which was still set each morning by the Reserve Bank. Money had rushed out of the country before the election, as markets punted that a new government would devalue the currency. The incoming government was immediately briefed by the Treasury on the state of the budget, which – surprise, surprise – was not what the outgoing government had claimed it was. This was the first of the Black Hole reveals.

The drama of the currency and a budget in disarray came to frame much of the government's first year, rather than the platform on which it had been elected. Labor was constantly battling the deep suspicions of business and financial markets about its economic management capacities, trying to prove that it was not another Whitlam government.

And here Hawke and the young politician who had been put into the job as treasurer just weeks before the election – and who had not been the author of the policies in that campaign – proved to be big surprises. Bob Hawke and Paul Keating floated the Australian dollar late in 1983 and accelerated a process begun grudgingly by Fraser at the behest of his ambitious treasurer, John Howard, to deregulate the financial system. Hawke and Keating's approach was driven by pragmatism, rather than any intense commitment to the free-market sentiment sweeping the world.

Sixteen months later, David Lange led New Zealand Labour to a smashing victory over Muldoon, who had perhaps unwisely set Bastille Day as election day. Across the Tasman, the parallels continued to be a little spooky – almost a borrowed playbook from Australia. There was an immediate currency crisis. As in Australia, foreign currency speculators had started selling the dollar when the election was called. But in New Zealand, the pressures for devaluation were not just about stopping the speculators. The massive borrowings of the previous decade and extraordinary levels of regulation of the economy meant that the value of the currency had become wildly distorted. The advice from New Zealand's central bank and the Treasury, long before the election, was that the currency should be devalued. Muldoon ignored them. When those same officials briefed Lange as the incoming prime minister, the advice was alarming.

"[Muldoon] did not tell me that the run on the dollar had almost used up the Reserve Bank's stock of foreign currency. Nor did he tell me that the country was close to the point of defaulting on its international obligations." Lange recalled how, in making the case for devaluation, the officials reported that "they had gone so far as to ask diplomatic posts overseas to find out how much foreign currency could be borrowed on credit cards. We were close to the edge."

Labour under Lange would devalue the currency by 20 per cent, remove controls on interest rates and freeze wages and prices for three months. These were, of course, radical steps to take. But Muldoon – the great regulator and controller of all things – had created such a sense of crisis that it made such changes seem absolutely necessary.

While the shock of the world suddenly looking very different to what was expected closely reflected the experiences of Labor in Australia just twelve months earlier, there are few signs that the possible lessons were registered in New Zealand. Here's the thing: despite all the similarities, those involved in the crisis in New Zealand didn't see it as a replica of the Australian experience, or even look to how Hawke and Keating responded. There are no references to Australia in the histories of the period. Those who worked inside the government seem a little surprised when you ask whether the Australian decisions had any influence.

Roger Douglas was Lange's finance minister. Unlike Hawke and Keating, he came to office with a detailed plan for radical free-market reform, dating from long before the 1984 election: to introduce a goods and services tax and a flat income-tax regime, and to greatly reduce the public sector. The Treasury and Reserve Bank – growing increasingly frustrated by Muldoon's policy interventions, and aware of the profound changes in economic thought and theory around the world – also had a clear view of where policy should go. On the Monday after the election, Douglas set out a detailed agenda to his officials. He saw that the sense of crisis amid which the government had come to office was "undoubtedly a great window of opportunity," which he ought to exploit by building a sense of momentum. "It got the ball rolling and in a sense I've made every endeavour to ensure the ball didn't stop rolling. I sort of had that principle that it was much harder to shoot me down if I kept one pace ahead."

It is sometimes commented in New Zealand that it was the momentum, rather than the actual reform agenda, that got all the attention. There was a particular deregulatory machismo abroad. Not only was Douglas different from Keating in that he came in with a very clear idea of what he was going to do, but the crisis had also increased the speed with which he could do it. Financial market deregulation was completed between the government's election in July 1984 and the beginning of March the next year – compared to a gradual process spread over four or five years in Australia – sparking an explosion in the financial markets, in bank lending, and in spivs very similar to the ones we saw in Australia.

In both countries, the deregulation of the financial markets – which superficially sounds so dull – created exhilaration and liberty in the business community, but also a looming and sudden sense of vulnerability to the judgment of the world. When Douglas unveiled his first budget, the cost of deregulation and of that vulnerability started to become clear. The huge subsidies to farmers were cut overnight. The first instalments of "Rogernomics" had been made. Much more was to come. Australians and New Zealanders were being confronted with new views of their futures. What had forged our past views of ourselves, and our views of each other, was our relationship with Britain.

At federation in 1901, there was a strong expectation that New Zealand would become one of the states of Australia. Section 6 of the *Commonwealth of Australia Constitution Act* refers to New Zealand as potentially a state in the new federation.

In the first half of the nineteenth century, the colony of New South Wales had acted as a sort of imperial liaison point between London and what was still not quite a colony across the Tasman, more a few outposts of whalers, escaped convicts and adventurers. Most of New Zealand had been included as part of the arbitrarily defined colony of New South Wales in Arthur Phillip's commission in 1787. However, there wasn't any official British administrative presence in New Zealand, and not even much interest in establishing one, until 1839, when London felt obliged to declare New South Wales' legal and court authority over the place. In fact, London obliged the colony of New South Wales to fund the establishment of New Zealand's first institutions. But by this time, simply making such declarations was not quite so simple. Māori had first declared sovereignty and independence (*He Whakaputanga*) in 1835, a declaration recognised by Britain, and then signed the Treaty of Waitangi in 1840, after attempts by traders to buy up large tracts of land prompted the British to try to persuade Māori to cede sovereignty over their lands.

Fast-forward to the end of the century and the push to federation in Australia. The federation discussion among the Australian colonies was fashioned by growing trade disputes among them and the potential benefits that becoming one country offered in defence against foreign invasion. Sir John Hall, then premier of New Zealand and one of two New Zealand delegates to the 1890 federation conference, argued that "any decision by New Zealand to enter federation would have to depend on an emerging 'community of interest' with the Australian colonies, and it must also be accompanied by a constitutional guarantee of the continuing independence of each constituent state, including an adequate degree of representation in the federal parliament."

But if security and free trade were the incentive, the reality was that New Zealand would still be distant from Australia's defences, and it would inevitably be paying taxes to a government running things from a long way away.

There was the countervailing concern that federation might result in Australian tariffs raised against New Zealand goods. Then there were all the questions about status and self-perception. For the Australian colonies, federation offered the prospect of becoming the head boy in the region: not just presiding over the Australian mainland and New Zealand, but also perhaps over other places in the Pacific, such as Fiji.

For New Zealand, the benefits were less clear. There were important differences in self-perception, which constitutional lawyer Nicholas Aroney notes included "a recurrent assertion that New Zealanders consti-tuted a superior 'British type', unblemished by the convict origins of New South Wales and Van Diemen's Land," and "a view that the status of the Māori was in some sense superior to the treatment received by Australia's indigenous peoples."

And it has to be remembered that the principal relationship both places valued was not with each other, but with Britain. What played a huge part in the way both the federating Australian colonies and New Zealand saw themselves, and assessed their relationship at this time, was refrigeration. The development of refrigerated shipping in the 1880s had transformed the markets and economies of both places, but particularly New Zealand's. Britain had become New Zealand's dominant trading partner. That gave the small country a sense of economic independence and confidence. But it also meant Australia and New Zealand were now rivals for the British market, as well as British goodwill.

And that particularly played out when it came to matters of warfare. There is no foundation myth more heavily entrenched, perhaps even overused in the Australian psyche, than that of Anzac and Gallipoli. It says a lot about us that we tend to see it as an Australian experience. When the Glebe Island Bridge in Sydney was officially renamed the Anzac Bridge on Remembrance

Day 1998, it was marked by the statue of a lone Australian digger. Someone had forgotten the New Zealanders. And it would be another eight years before a statue of a Kiwi soldier was added. (The two soldiers look away from each other.)

In his book *The Prickly Pear*, long-serving New Zealand diplomat Denis McLean gives a fascinating Kiwi perspective, noting that "the Australians fashioned the ANZAC legend out of Australian clay from the outset. Even in late December 1915, only days after the evacuation from the Dardanelles, Major-General I.G. McKay, speaking at the Melbourne Town Hall, had no doubt but that ANZAC and Australia were synonymous." He declared:

> The first great sacred spot in the history of Australia was the ANZAC beach and the heights above it ... There were 20,000 of us on a 380-acre selection for several months, under fire all the time. Small as it was, that bit of Gallipoli would forever be part of Australia.

McLean writes that "New Zealanders' exasperation with such Australian self-absorption and conceits would become a large element of their own sense of identity. It has remained so. Many were bitter."

Despite this, Gallipoli also remains at the centre of any sentimental kinship we claim with New Zealand. Yet there is some irony in the fact that the soldiers of the two new countries had such a low opinion of each other. McLean notes that Australia's official war historian, C.E.W. Bean, considered New Zealanders "colourless." "Australians tended to think of New Zealanders as a 'pale imitation' of themselves," McLean writes. "A New Zealand trooper's judgement of Australians in general would have found a wide echo among his compatriots": "The Australian, and more especially the town-bred man, is a skiting bumptious fool who thinks nobody knows anything but himself."

In a revealing, and not at all flattering, reflection, this trooper went on to say that: "Australians tended to think the New Zealanders were 'soft on the blacks.' They were far too inclined to treat them as they would a Māori, without recognising that New Zealanders were demeaning themselves by not recognising that the 'gyppo' was a lesser being on the human scale."

By contrast, McLean says, "New Zealand national myth was still centred on the conceit that New Zealand was the most favoured of the British dominions and New Zealanders were the 'select' among overseas Britons. They felt no need for swagger. Their identity as New Zealanders was plain to them; they were, apart from anything else, not Australians."

From the carnage of the First World War, "New Zealanders and Australians would each hew out new estimates of themselves. What emerged was a maimed nationhood for each, rather than any deep-rooted sense of collective identity. Gallipoli and the first ANZACs have left a confused legacy, at once a kind of blood brotherhood and prideful separate nationalisms."

Yet on formal occasions, it is always Gallipoli, and the myth-making it generated, that modern political leaders put at the heart of the relationship.

"Our ties were indelibly forged in hardship and mateship, from Gallipoli and the Somme to Tobruk, Korea and beyond," Australian Prime Minister Julia Gillard told the New Zealand parliament in 2011. New Zealand Prime Minister John Key demonstrated a slightly less ghoulish view of his countrymen about the great myth when he addressed the Australian parliament later that year. He began his speech in the present, and in gratitude for assistance given after the devastating Christchurch earthquake that year. But then there was reference to "indelible common values [that] we have fought for together. As joint forces in Gallipoli and as fellow soldiers in other theatres of war, from the First and Second World Wars through to Korea and Vietnam. The experiences we shared in these battles shaped our national characters. They joined us ever unto each other."

It says a lot that we still seem to define our relationship with New Zealand by these historic experiences of defence, not by a political, economic or cultural shared history or a relationship that once saw us almost become one country, or indeed the modern reality that we have the closest economic relationship of any two countries on earth.

Federation and Gallipoli tell us much about our shared history and myths. But they don't necessarily tell us about our separate histories, and the legacies these have left, particularly that of the treatment of indigenous people. In the past fifty years, both Australia and New Zealand have been confronted with these legacies and the need to address them, more so than at any time in the past. But with very different results.

Each country's starting point was also very different. Australia — as a nation — came into being with an act of the British parliament and a constitution which contained no rousing words or aspirations, just a series of tightly negotiated arrangements for how the colonies would get on with each other. Since the new country had been established on the legal idea of terra nullius — that it was unoccupied land when the British arrived — no thought was given to negotiating a treaty with the original inhabitants, nor later to recognising them in the constitution.

Things could not have been more different in New Zealand. The Treaty of Waitangi (Te Tiriti o Waitangi) — considered the country's founding document — even predated the formal establishment of a colony. It was a negotiation between the Crown and around 540 Māori chiefs on the North Island.

In fact, New Zealand still doesn't have a constitution as Australians know it. The parliament only passed its own Constitution Act in 1986; this overrode an ability for the British parliament to pass laws for New Zealand without consent. The 1986 act can be changed at any time by the parliament, without a referendum. Like Australia's constitution, perhaps even more so, it is written as a matter-of-fact piece of law, going to the respective powers of the Crown, the parliament and the judiciary. Nothing aspirational to see here.

For different reasons, neither Australia's constitution nor New Zealand's Constitution Act has anything to say about the circumstances of the country when it came to be formed, nor who was here already and might therefore have desired a say in what happened next. Between terra nullius and the Treaty of Waitangi, it is hard to think of more opposite circumstances in which two places were settled, or in which the position of indigenous people would be considered.

Indigenous people in both countries came off badly, in both their circumstances and their legal standing. Yet there is an extraordinary relevance in how the Treaty of Waitangi has developed in the last half-century to the debate we are now having in Australia about Indigenous recognition and a Voice to Parliament. And to a debate we have generally not been having about truth-telling and reconciliation.

What New Zealand gives us is a slightly different prism through which to observe the positive value these things can bring to a country without undoing it. For the past quarter of a century, Australia has been stuck in a quagmire when it comes to the question of the status and rights – as citizens – of Indigenous people. Issues of inequality, incarceration, injustice, shorter life expectancies, and poorer health and education outcomes haven't moved either. We don't even have an organising principle, odious or otherwise, with which to consider these issues.

But if there is one area where there was reason to expect change, an area which should have provoked a fundamental rethink, it was in the legal recognition of Indigenous people and their rights. In 1992, the High Court's *Mabo* judgment overturned *terra nullius*. Title to land has usually had a strong correlation to people's rights to have a say. British voting rights – and the voting rights of systems founded on English law – were long based on property titles. But early expectations that the *Mabo* judgment could lead to great change were thwarted.

There was goodwill in the beginning, although government and Indigenous leaders struggled with the wicked legal complexities presented by the judgment. In its wake, negotiations took place between the parliament and Indigenous representatives to give status in legislation to the concept of native title to land. Although the British have long had "customs in common," native title was not a concept of English law. It recognised rights and interests to land coming from traditional laws and customs: the right to live on a particular piece of land; or to access it for traditional purposes, such as camping or ceremonies; or to hunt, fish and gather food or resources, such as water, wood and ochre; or to teach traditional law and customs. After *Mabo*, there were even some native title cases that gave the right to possession and occupancy to the exclusion of all others on vacant Crown land, including the right to prevent others accessing and using land – a potentially threatening decision for mining exploration and development. Pastoral leases – which cover broad swathes of the continent inland – were found by the court not to extinguish native title.

A body was set up – the National Native Title Tribunal – to consider claims for title. But the idea of compensating people for a loss of title to their land was not really on the agenda: the act only allowed for compensation for loss of title after 1975.

Then, in 1996, the High Court was asked to consider the native title question further in the case of the *Wik Peoples v. The State of Queensland*. The Court found that the pastoral leases under consideration did not give exclusive rights to the leaseholder and, as a result, native title could coexist on pastoral leases.

But there had been a change of government, and a change of mood. Instead of forward progress, the new government was leading a backlash against Indigenous people, against what the new prime minister, John Howard, called the "black armband" view of history.

The body set up by the Labor government in 1990 with the ambition of giving a voice to Indigenous people, the Aboriginal and Torres Strait Islander Commission, was abolished in 2005. There was much that had proved deeply flawed in its operations, and in its ambitions to be representative. But it had also only been in operation for a few years. Other Aboriginal bodies were immediately tainted by implications of corruption and incompetence. Most importantly, there was no road map to what, if anything, would replace it. The question of how to fund remote Indigenous communities, or even whether they needed special help, became inflammatory amid usually poorly informed debate. The issues that had been highlighted by ATSIC's existence – the mishmash of federal and state funding, particularly for housing and health – were never resolved. Income support became mixed up with broader debates about "mutual obligation" and "work for the dole." The underlying rationale of government policy got stuck somewhere between the old policies of assimilation, self-determination and crisis management.

The new mood set the backdrop for public reaction to the *Wik* case. What followed was quite a lot of hysteria, which the government inflamed rather than soothed. Giant maps showing how much land was "under threat" were held up at press conferences. There were dark warnings that people's suburban backyards, along with their Hills Hoists, were exposed to claims. This was despite the High Court finding that where there was conflict, the rights under the pastoral lease would extinguish remaining native title rights.

Subsequent legislation provided "security of tenure" to pastoral lease holders and placed restrictions on native title claims. The legislation to close down the impact of the *Wik* judgment as much as possible, Pauline Hanson's debut on the national political stage and the later closure of ATSIC marked the beginning of a long period in which constructive discussion of Indigenous issues was deposited in a back corner of the national cupboard, like some of the ephemera of moving house which you can't quite work out what to do with.

There was remorse and horror over the report of the national inquiry into children stolen from their families and, eventually, a national apology. There was an ambition to "Close the Gap" between white and black Australia. But little actually happened. It seemed that "something like a cult of forgetfulness practised on a national scale," as anthropologist W.E.H. Stanner had described in 1968, once more took hold when it came to political discussion of the rights of Indigenous people.

It was only in the area of native title that things seemed to keep moving quietly forward in the legal system, even if it was largely out of sight of most Australians. Claims continued to be made in the National Native Title Tribunal and new ground was slowly gained about what it represented. Significant High Court cases in the past couple of years have changed the nature of the native title debate, most notably the Timber Creek case, which saw the focus shift from establishing whether native title still existed, to compensation. The original *Native Title Act* in 1993 had only spoken of (undefined) "just terms" compensation.

In early 2020, there was another significant decision when the Yamatji Nation was awarded both non-exclusive possession rights as part of native title recognition and a $450 million package, for a claim to an area covering nearly 48,000 square kilometres of Western Australia.

As native title — in at least some parts of Australia — has been plodding along its complex and legalistic path over the past twenty-five years, there has been a concomitant process in New Zealand.

Ever since the Treaty of Waitangi was signed in 1840, it has been the subject of hot dispute, starting with different translations of what exactly both sides meant by it. Māori argued it was supposed to be a partnership, a sharing.

> The version written in Māori — was an "essential exchange" between the partners: the Crown was ceded the right to establish civil government ("*kawanatanga*" in article 1) in exchange for guaranteeing to Māori the continued 'chieftainship' of their lands, estates and treasures ("*rangatiratanga o ratou wenua, o ratou kainga me o ratou taonga katoa*" in article 2).

The colonists who arrived in increasing numbers — and then their government — did not see it that way. The treaty was repeatedly breached: the government cheated Māori by buying land at ridiculously low prices; or just confiscated it or conned them out of it by other means. It stripped them of their rights to fish through regulation and assumed ownership of rivers and lakes.

Australian lawyer Shireen Morris describes the impact of underlying attitudes:

> Views that saw the Maori as an inferior race led courts in 1877 to declare the Treaty legally invalid. The racially discriminatory attitudes

of the era viewed the Maori as "savages" and "uncivilised barbarians," not possessing any sovereignty prior to colonisation. Accordingly, Maori were considered politically incapable of having entered into a valid Treaty with the Crown and were deemed incapable of retaining rights to land and property.

As Morris notes, "The discriminatory logic of *terra nullius* initially prevailed in New Zealand, as it did in Australia, despite the Treaty." But this meant that, in the country that became New Zealand, the Crown's word was being broken. And it has always been the Crown's word, not the government's, that matters. The treaty was between Queen Victoria and the tribal chiefs.

But whatever various courts might have said in the intervening period, the treaty was a public historical document which acknowledged Maori prior possession of lands, forests and fisheries. And the sheer force of its existence would come back into play by the middle of the last century, as a mass movement of Māori to the cities and increasing Māori political activism challenged the status quo.

In 1975, just as change was starting to sweep through the country in the wake of Britain's decision to join the European Common Market, New Zealand established the Waitangi Tribunal to consider modern-day breaches of the treaty. At first, this was more an idea in theory rather than a practical body, but it quickly developed into a push for recognition of contemporary events with historical roots.

Bastion Point in Auckland was one of the most famous early cases. The land had been taken from the Ngāti Whātua for military use in the 1950s, but the iwi (tribe) expected the land to be returned when it was no longer needed for this. In 1977, the government instead announced plans to develop the site for high-income housing. Protests and occupation followed. In February 1978, the government offered to return some land and houses if the iwi paid $200,000 in development costs. The occupiers, led by Joe Hawke of the Ōrākei Māori Action Committee, stayed put, but on 25 May – 506 days after they had arrived – a large troop of police moved to evict them, arresting 222 protesters and demolishing buildings. When the jurisdiction of the Waitangi Tribunal was widened to cover retrospective issues, Hawke's Ōrākei claim was the first historical claim to be heard. The tribunal's 1987 report recommended the return of land to Ngāti Whātua, and the following year the government agreed.

The tribunal has gradually evolved to being a lot more than a basic land titles court. Through it, Māori (re)gained fishing rights, rights to water and even to radio bandwidth. But the tribunal has also become the path to truth and reconciliation for the country: it documents grievances, stories and histories. One New Zealand writer noted how, as hearings on claims progressed, the tribunal's reports "began to sketch a historical backdrop which had largely been hidden from the eyes of ordinary New Zealanders[, as] case by case there was an examination of injustices that had never been resolved ... nor openly admitted."

But there has been more. The tribunal helped establish the standing of the Māori language, as both a cultural treasure protected under the treaty and an official language. The New Zealand National Geographic Board gives dual names to places. While the parliament declined in 2019 to a legal name change, it is commonplace in New Zealand, including in government and in pieces of legislation, to refer to the country by its Māori name: Aotearoa. Māori culture is increasingly seen as New Zealand's culture. Consider how the *haka* has been adopted by *pākehā* (white New Zealanders) in New Zealand; its power when performed spontaneously by schoolchildren in the wake of the 2019 Christchurch massacre; and that the New Zealand prime minister wears a Māori ceremonial cloak on occasions of great national moment.

It was not that this process was without considerable political contention, nor was it perfect. But there was a sense that New Zealanders came to see treaty settlements as something that just had to be done.

The man who drafted the laws in 1985 allowing claims to go back to 1840 was constitutional lawyer and later Labour prime minister Geoffrey Palmer. He noted that:

it was greatly resisted at the time, and I never got as much mail opposing anything as when we did that. People hated the idea. There was a lot of racism in New Zealand then. [People] just felt that the Maori shouldn't have these things. The Treaty was old and we shouldn't take any notice of it now. That it was part of history. A tremendous lot of opposition to that. But actually, it has worked out better. And we've had various hiccups … It is a great credit to the National Party that they … went on doing the settlements, because like our system of government that the public doesn't really understand properly, they didn't understand the settler government injustices that were inflicted on Maori during the nineteenth century. They were absolutely legion, these injustices. The confiscation of land, the sharks taking away the land of Maori. And the settlements that have been reached do provide some sort of remedy for what was injustice. When I first got into politics, people said, "the Treaty is a fraud." They don't say that now.

Compare this with how our current prime minister is sidling away from even the small progress of making a Welcome to Country a standard part of official events: Morrison has downgraded it by grouping it with a greeting to defence veterans at the beginning of every speech.

In New Zealand, acknowledging the treaty became bipartisan. National Prime Minister Jim Bolger, who came to office in 1990 after the government of which Palmer was a member fell apart, began the process of negotiating significant Waitangi settlements. "In the early days … the [protest] slogans were 'the Treaty is a fraud,' and that was a strong campaign for a few years," he said in 2016.

> On reflection, of course, they were absolutely right, because what the Treaty promised hadn't been delivered. To that extent it was a fraud. Then the slogan of protest shifted to "Honour the Treaty," which is really where I think you could say the work that I and others have done has moved to take New Zealand with us to honour the Treaty; the commitments that were entered into.

And what we're really talking about is New Zealand's honour. I mean, people try to get the words – "Will they mean a bit of this? Will they mean a bit of that?" But there is no question what the intent was. That there should be a respect and understanding and acknowledgement that Maori were here first, that they own the assets of the land.

Honour. It feels like it's been a while since we've heard that word thrown around in Australian politics. Or even considered the concept of national honour.

There would be three landmark Waitangi settlements settled, or initiated, by Bolger. One claim – that of the Ngāi Tahu – covered much of the South Island. Another gave Māori a substantial interest in the country's fishing business and fish quota system. They were significant financial concessions – though, it must be acknowledged, they hardly represented all that had been lost.

As in Australia over the implications for landholders of the *Mabo* and *Wik* judgments, there was alarm and backlash to the deals. The National party room was getting anxious as the 1996 election approached, but Bolger held firm, noting that, "Māori were going to continue to live as they are until they got the settlement done properly and then they'd move forward."

Bolger also advocated the teaching of *te reo Māori* (language) in schools, talked a lot about identity, agreed to consider renaming New Zealand Aotearoa, and was a driving force behind establishing Te Papa Tongarewa as the national museum (the name means "container of treasures"). It replaced what had first been the Colonial Museum, then the Dominion Museum. "We needed a museum that captured who we were as a people, as a nation, as a country," he said.

Waitangi Tribunal settlements involve financial and cultural redress and recognition, as well as official apologies from the Crown for past breaches. There have been controversial cases involving access to beaches, rivers and fishing rights. And race, as an issue in politics, has raised its ugly head in New Zealand, just as it has in Australia.

Race flared regularly as a political issue during the Howard years, most spectacularly with the arrival of Pauline Hanson in federal parliament. It often contaminated other contentious issues, such as asylum seeker policy. The major parties frequently chose not to confront it directly. There were often accusations of dog-whistle politics.

In Australia in 2005, we witnessed the ugly spectacle of the Cronulla riots. In December, 5000 people descended on Cronulla Beach in Sydney, chanting racist slogans and attacking people of Middle Eastern appearance. Prime Minister Howard condemned the race-based attacks, but said the next day, "I do not accept there is underlying racism in this country."

During its second term in office, from 2002 and 2005, the NZ Labour coalition government led by Helen Clark found itself faced with a National push towards Hanson-esque race politics. A court judgment in 2003 – similar in many ways to the *Mabo* and *Wik* cases in Australia – had raised the spectre that Māori could lay claim to the entire foreshore and seabed of New Zealand. Clark announced legislation to ensure the foreshore and seabed would be vested in the Crown, but with scope for Māori consultation. Bitter debate ensued – both from Māori, who protested extinguishment of rights, and from the National Opposition, which claimed Māori were getting rights over and above those of other New Zealanders.

If the issue was not already contentious enough, the then National leader, Don Brash – a former governor of the Reserve Bank of New Zealand – gave a speech in 2004 which other prime ministers have since likened to the language of Donald Trump. He certainly pressed many of the same buttons as Howard, with his "black armband" view of history, and as Hanson. Brash spoke of the "dangerous drift towards racial separatism in New Zealand, and the development of the now entrenched Treaty grievance industry." He voiced non-Māori resentment at having to pay compensation for a nineteenth-century treaty they didn't sign, and questioned the idea that Māori were more heavily represented among New Zealand's poor.

> None of us was around at the time of the New Zealand wars. None
> of us had anything to do with the confiscations. There is a limit to

how much any generation can apologise for the sins of its great-grandparents ... Too many of us look back through utopian glasses, imagining the Polynesian past as a genteel world of "wise ecologists, mystical sages, gifted artists, heroic navigators and pacifists who wouldn't hurt a fly." It was nothing like that. Life was hard, brutal and short.

The speech resonated with many New Zealanders and put the government under pressure. Brash enjoyed a seventeen-point rise in the polls. Clark did not confront Brash about it at the time and this became one of the issues for which her prime ministership was eventually marked down by voters. Her response is a pragmatic one. "You know, can you do more for New Zealand – including Māori – out of government or in government?" she asked in 2016. "You're not going to change the policies that are lifting Māori, so how politically are you going to manage this problem? And in the end we came through it, but it was a very unpleasant set of forces that he unleashed, which we somehow had to overcome."

It is noteworthy that the very attempt to achieve historical settlements is valued by New Zealand's prime ministers, no matter how much they got right or wrong. John Key, prime minister of the conservative National government between 2008 and 2016, regarded getting settlements completed as one of his greatest legacies, as did some assessments of his period in office.

The Waitangi Tribunal now hears and resolves historical breaches of the treaty going back to 1840. New Zealand has taken a more serious approach than Australia to compensation. The Ngāi Tahu claim was settled with a statement of recognition of the relationship of the iwi with their land, but also a cash settlement and the return of property. A sense of reconciliation also started to emerge in the process. In this particular claim, it was agreed that Mount Cook would be formally renamed Aoraki / Mount Cook. It would be returned to Ngāi Tahu, to be gifted back to the people of New Zealand.

"Economic losses to Ngāi Tahu from the Crown's land purchases of the last century were valued at more than $20 billion," the tribe's website notes. "The Crown's Settlement Offer of $170 million was clearly much less than this amount. However, in deciding whether the Crown's Settlement Offer was acceptable, it was important to ask: 'Was the offer "sufficient" to re-establish the tribe's economic base, in order for it to fund the social development of Ngāi Tahu?'"

Some of the settlements have been big: big enough to cause alarm. It made putting a finite cap and time limit on claims a political issue for some years. The Crown committed to reaching a final settlement with each Māori tribe, with each settlement intended to be a resolution of all historical grievances, so that the Māori and the Crown can move forward together in a constructive partnership for the future.

The settlements do not offer full compensation for loss but instead a form of redress, which recognises the grievance and contributes to future economic development. As of 2018, they amounted to around NZ$2.2 billion, although a consultancy firm valued the assets of Māori "post-settlement entities" at NZ$7.8 billion, suggesting the settlements have been used to increase the wealth of the iwi who made them.

Academics Nicola Wheen and Janine Hayward note the process has "divided public opinion: it is lauded as a tremendous achievement and criticised as a 'gravy train' for lawyers."

> Opinions differ on who benefits most from Treaty settlements: an elite Māori few, or all Māori with access to the economic base resulting from settlement. It has been the subject of much debate in Parliament and the subject of litigation in the courts. The settlement process has attracted international attention from nations attempting to address the grievances of Indigenous peoples. While most New Zealanders may have an opinion on Treaty settlements, they may also lack an understanding of why Treaty settlements are required and what the process seeks to achieve.

The treaty's original recognition of land rights did not stop Māori being impoverished and left without land. But New Zealand's attempts since the

1980s to redress its own failures to honour the treaty involved not only setting up an institutional process to deal with claims, but also a shift in the standing of the issue in the national political debate.

*

The Treaty of Waitangi represented much more than just the recognition of possession of land. Article 3 of the treaty gave Māori the rights and privileges of British subjects, almost 130 years before Indigenous Australians were counted in the Australian population.

Māori were given four dedicated seats in the parliament – originally elected from a separate electoral roll. This sounds pretty advanced until you consider they were in the majority at the time, not the minority.

For an Australian observer, there is much that leaps out of the history of Māori issues over the past fifty years, particularly the way the tribunal process has developed and, along the way, changed the cultural and political nature of New Zealand.

Three things seem particularly clear. The first is the power of structures that give indigenous people a say: structures that don't have to be all that threatening to the rest of the community. The establishment of the Waitangi Tribunal in 1975 – and its later development into a body that considered past treaty breaches, not just contemporary ones – meant there was a structure in place through which histories could be documented. The four Māori seats in parliament had played an important role in this, because it was a Māori MP, Matiu Rata, who pushed to establish the tribunal. The New Zealand Māori Council – a representative body with deep roots back to the 1800s, but which was formally recognised and had its functions articulated in legislation in 1962 – also helped Māori organise and articulate their predicament.

The second thing that emerges is that with recognition of wrongs there also came recognition of the value of culture. The debate didn't just become about a past wiped out, but about keeping alive a culture into the present.

Finally, there is the power of truth-telling, of issues resolved, for a country.

When you think of these lessons from New Zealand, you realise that what is at stake are the key elements of the Uluru Statement from the Heart – but with the benefit of seeing them from a different perspective, one where everything you have heard is impossible has already happened, and proved completely possible.

The powerful language of the Uluru Statement – which emerged from a meeting of Indigenous people from across Australia in 2017 – sparkled and dazzled, then seemed to be doused almost instantly by politicians implying it involved a "third chamber of parliament." Something the statement never sought. It asked for constitutional reform and a Makarrata Commission: "Makarrata is the culmination of our agenda: the coming together after a struggle. It captures our aspirations for a fair and truthful relationship with the people of Australia and a better future for our children based on justice and self-determination."

Indigenous Australian academic Megan Davis observed earlier this year that the Uluru Statement "was a game-changer."

> If treaty was the British Crown's solution to dispossession elsewhere, the Uluru statement is the Australian solution to a very Australian problem. The dialogues sought to inject the one thing that had been decoupled from the recognition process: truth-telling about Australian history. Uluru reoriented Australian reconciliation to where it should be: what is the truth and what does repair look like? The reform agenda spoke to Voice, Makarrata and Truth.

The statement was not prescriptive about the nature of constitutional reform, just about what it wanted to be achieved: something that addresses "the structural nature of our problem." And that problem is "our powerlessness."

A sovereignty that had been recognised in the High Court decisions "has never been ceded or extinguished, and co-exists with the sovereignty of the Crown."

With substantive constitutional change and structural reform, we believe this ancient sovereignty can shine through as a fuller expression of Australia's nationhood ... We seek constitutional reforms to empower our people and take a *rightful place* in our own country. When we have power over our destiny our children will flourish. They will walk in two worlds and their culture will be a gift to their country.

The statement called for "the establishment of a First Nations Voice enshrined in the Constitution." People have been brawling about what that actually means ever since, just as they have been brawling about what "recognition" in the constitution would mean.

Reflecting in 2015, two years before the Uluru Statement, on lessons Australians could take from New Zealand, Shireen Morris noted that the Treaty of Waitangi:

established important standing and rights for Maori and was crucial to the development of institutional structures to recognise and give Maori a voice in New Zealand's political system. It came to be seen as the foundation for a positive re-calibration of the relationship between Maori people and the Crown; it is now said to establish biculturalism, a principle of partnership between Maori and the state, and a duty to negotiate reasonably and in good faith. These principles have become ingrained. The fiduciary principle has emerged as a duty to consult which, though not legally actionable, has developed moral and political force. Treaty principles are now incorporated into several pieces of legislation.

*

There are still plenty of flaws in New Zealand's dealings with its Indigenous people. But what has happened there – the fact that it has been possible to establish, as Morris says, a mostly comfortable biculturalism, must give us scope to consider to what extent our own sense of maimed nationhood lurks not far beneath the surface. There has long been a debate that surges in negative waves and then subsides again as we explore our capacity for difference. We celebrate multiculturalism in Australia. Why is it so much harder for us to embrace this extraordinary, ancient culture, let alone acknowledge the hard legal realities that our courts have recognised in our history?

Why is there so little discussion of the idea of Australia acting in an "honourable" way? Why is it that we can't seem even to imagine a sense of partnership with Indigenous people in settling history and dealing with our modern problems?

There is a history going back into the earliest days of the colony – documented by the early governors – of Indigenous people being prepared to share the resources of the land. Extraordinary acts of grace against invaders. And in the Uluru Statement, we non-Indigenous Australians were offered another chance, another proposal to be gracious, and to share. And we comprehensively stuffed it.

Of course, representative structures and truth-telling do not of themselves address all the complex problems of Indigenous communities, let alone their disadvantage, even if they may ultimately help in finding ways out of it. Māori face greater disadvantage than pākehā on a wide range of measures. But it is to Australia's shame that they are nowhere near the levels of disadvantage experienced by Indigenous Australians. Direct comparisons are difficult, but a 2017 paper from the Centre for Aboriginal Economic Policy Research on the comparative wellbeing of Māori and Indigenous Australians gives us some not too subtle pointers. The paper compared the relative position of Indigenous and non-Indigenous peoples in each country. It found that the Māori employment rate is substantially higher than that of Indigenous Australians. Both Māori and Indigenous Australian households have much lower incomes than non-indigenous households. But the gap in household incomes is much larger in Australia than in New Zealand. Indigenous Australians have a higher imprisonment rate than Māori, and the difference has increased substantially since 2000.

In both New Zealand and Australia, the indigenous imprisonment rate is many times higher than the non-indigenous rate. A crucial point that emerges in the paper is the link between economic growth and progress for indigenous peoples. That is, when you start from a position of disadvantage, you are likely to be the first hit when things go bad. Alternatively, the good times offer the best chance of improving your employment and other prospects.

One of the biggest political and economic stories in New Zealand in the past forty years has been growing inequality, which has hit Māori particularly hard. This has largely been the outcome of conscious policy choices by various governments. And it is to the story of how and why those choices were made that we turn next.

The strangest thing about the Australia–New Zealand relationship is that our strongest link is the one we seem to talk about least. Our strongest link is actually our economic link. Most Australians know or talk little of it, except when some particular policy initiative by New Zealand becomes fodder for Australia's political debate.

"Shared history, values and institutions, personal connections, geographical proximity and a healthy sporting rivalry combine to make New Zealand's relationship with Australia our closest and most significant," begins the official Kiwi blurb on the bilateral relationship. "We also work together in virtually every area of government, including on trade and economic issues, and in defence and foreign policy." The same tone is mirrored in the Australian version: "Australia and New Zealand are natural allies with a strong trans-Tasman sense of family. Migration, trade and defence ties, keen competition on the sporting field, and strong people-to-people links have helped shape a close and co-operative relationship." The fact that we share "the world's most comprehensive, effective and mutually compatible free trade agreement" is recognised further on in the Kiwi patter. And okay, it sounds a little dull.

But despite New Zealand's decision not to join the federation in 1901, the country is our closest economic partner, and we are the Kiwis' most significant such partner.

China may have come to dominate the exports of both countries in the past couple of decades, but close to 15 per cent of New Zealand's population – according to a New Zealand cabinet paper from early 2020, around 650,000 New Zealand citizens – live in Australia, while around 70,000 Australians live in New Zealand. Since 1983, tariffs have been removed between the two countries, and food and professional qualifications standards unified. The New Zealand banking system is dominated by Australia's big four banks, and Australia is a massive investor in New Zealand. New Zealand ministers take part in Australian federal and state councils to discuss how services are delivered in both countries. It's something the European Union could only dream of, really.

The perpetual penchant for competitiveness in the relationship means that, while Australians remain (speaking frankly) fairly oblivious of our economic relationship with New Zealand, we have looked there at crucial moments to see what they are doing and if it is somehow "better" than what we are deciding to do. The shame is that we usually haven't gone back to see how things turned out.

Australia was particularly mindful of what was going on in New Zealand during the first wave of deregulatory frenzy in the 1980s, when "Rogernomics" was in full swing. The Kiwis were cutting taxes more aggressively, privatising with greater abandon and cutting government spending harder, right at the time when the push to cut taxes and spending, and to privatise, was strong in Australia. "Why can't we just do what they are doing across the Tasman?" was the cry that rang out from those pushing for more and more change.

New Zealand has remained a stellar example for those wanting less government, less tax and more markets ever since. And this is what makes the story of its political and economic path of recent decades so important to understand. Even if it has not always been obvious, what has gone on across the Tasman has had a continuing deep influence on the conservative economic agenda in Australia.

To take just one example: after the global financial crisis, the federal Coalition prosecuted a relentless case against the Rudd and Gillard governments, arguing that Labor's response to the global financial crisis (GFC) had been an exercise in unnecessary budgetary profligacy. Tony Abbott, then leader of the Opposition, argued in 2010:

> There are other countries which have chosen a different path and there's no evidence that their response has been any less effective than ours. For instance, in New Zealand they have tried to reform their way through the global financial crisis under the new [National] government's leadership [of Prime Minister John Key] and they seem to be doing pretty well.

Similarly, Shadow Treasurer Joe Hockey responded to the 2013 budget by asking Treasurer Wayne Swan in parliament:

> How can the Australian treasurer insist that the government's budget of deficits, higher unemployment and slower economic growth is unavoidable when New Zealand has been able to deliver an earlier surplus without a major resources industry and a strong New Zealand dollar?

(Swan countered by noting, quite reasonably, that, unlike Australia, New Zealand had actually been in a recession, with lower growth, and had increased the rate of its goods and services tax.)

The economist John Quiggin wrote during 2013 that Abbott's and Hockey's remarks "reflect a consistent pattern over the past thirty years."

> During most of this period New Zealand has favoured free-market economic policies. Advocates of these policies have consistently predicted superior economic outcomes. In the early 1990s, for example, the late P.P. McGuinness suggested that New Zealand "shows every sign of being on the brink of overtaking Australia perhaps before the centenary of Federation in terms of living standards and economic performance."

The Abbott and Hockey view, and their reading of New Zealand policy prescriptions, came to shape their first budget in government, the budget of 2014. It is remembered mostly as a political disaster, but of course it was a direct and tangible disaster for particular individuals and sectors of the economy. Subsequent governments spent years trying to reverse the damage done, but you can never quite put things back as they were.

Which is what a lot of Kiwis would tell you about their own experience of radical and ideologically pig-headed budget cuts.

Contrary to the picture drawn by Abbott and Hockey, the numbers tell a very different and brutal story about what happened in the New Zealand economy. New Zealand has not – as Paddy McGuiness prophesied – overtaken

Australia in terms of living standards and economic performance. The Kiwi economy produces, and earns, way less per person than Australia. Incomes have fallen behind Australia's. The country has remained vulnerable to much more volatile swings than Australia. Inequality has risen sharply.

True, New Zealand has at times run much bigger budget surpluses than Australia's (as a proportion of the economy), and that has clearly contributed to cutting government debt. But for the past five years or so, it has been spending about the same amount on government services as Australia. The nicest complexion you can put on the comparative performance of the two economies is that, as we both sat on the edge of pandemic abyss at the beginning of 2020, some of the measures of our economic and budgetary performance were about the same. However, the cost in social disruption and dysfunction of getting to that point for New Zealand has been much, much greater.

When Rogernomics was in full swing in 1988, I spent time in New Zealand reporting to Australia on what was happening and why it was that they seemed to be getting "more" done.

Back at home, everyone in politics and the media seemed to have got on board the deregulation express. First, it had been macroeconomic changes, such as floating the dollar and cutting government spending. By 1987, the Hawke government had moved on to microeconomic reform: the restructuring of individual markets, such as telecommunications and transport. Such was the frenzy that, by 1989, then treasurer Keating famously complained, "I'll guarantee if you walk into any pet shop in Australia, what the resident galah will be talking about is microeconomic policy."

But it is one thing to pursue radical reform, another one to have it made law. Advocates of reform in Australia in the 1980s had already seen Keating's "Option C" tax proposal – for a consumption tax – defeated when the Hawke government chose to get consensus on tax reform at a summit with business, union and community leaders. In their eyes, Roger Douglas's "crash-through" style had a lot to recommend it, and there was much interest in just how it was that it seemed so easy to get reform through across the Tasman.

As we have seen, the political structure in New Zealand created huge power for the prime minister of the day, whether that be Piggy Muldoon or David Lange and his impatient finance minister. It wasn't that these measures weren't controversial. There was alarm and opposition to many of them. But the answer given to all who questioned the policy prescription came to be known as TINA: "there is no alternative."

The fact there was only one chamber of parliament, and no states, was certainly part of the story. The usual structural reasons given in Australia for why more got done was that New Zealand didn't have a Senate, and didn't have states to "get in the way" or make things more complicated. But that misses a crucial aspect of the Rogernomics era: the role of players and networks on the broader political stage. This gives us cause to reflect on the institutional forces at play in some of our own policy debates.

Douglas's policies were not a copy of Australia's, but a manifesto he had developed with a close cohort in the New Zealand Treasury and the Reserve Bank. Within the parliamentary party he had key like-minded allies. But it was the extra-parliamentary group who locked in support for these changes across crucial interest groups.

When Labour won the July 1984 election, Treasury presented it with a briefing paper titled *Economic Management*, which was an uncanny reflection of Douglas's thinking. The head of the NZ union movement later revealed that Douglas had outlined in a private briefing to unions six months earlier "his economic program[,] which was exactly what subsequently emerged."

> That program in February identified the GST, the movement to flat tax, the corporatisation/privatisation agenda, the 20 per cent devaluation.
>
> When we confronted David Lange and Geoffrey Palmer, they disavowed any support or knowledge of this, said it was a fabrication. When we objected to that they said it was a misunderstanding and we were requested to destroy all copies of this document . . .

The tragedy is that the union movement knew about it, and the union movement accepted the assurances of people like David Lange and Geoffrey Palmer that it wasn't their agenda.

Helen Clark, who fifteen years later would become prime minister, was on the Labour Party Executive at the same time.

We knew where Roger was going, right? And in the end, Geoffrey Palmer, who was a great draughtsman, was brought in to write a policy which could have meant anything ... and did. It was vague. It was fudged. It was fudged. Because the party could not agree with the direction Roger wanted to go ... And the policy that voters were reading is meaningless.

When you hear or read comments like this one, it is hard not be struck by the cheery resignation of Labour figures to the fact that they were, at best, keeping voters in the dark, or at worst lying to them. Maybe it was that everyone was vaguely thinking Douglas would not ultimately prevail, that some sort of compromise could be reached.

Muldoon's decision to call a snap election meant that any belief within Labour ranks that these issues might be sorted out before the election became irrelevant. But there was also something of an unholy trade-off made by Lange: delivering a hardline position on anti-nuclear issues to the left of his party in exchange for giving his finance minister control over an economic debate which had never much interested the prime minister anyway.

Two months after it was elected in 1984, the Labour government called an economic summit − but it was a complete stunt. The party president was Margaret Wilson. She recalled that she "was not invited to the summit and when I suggested that this was an oversight, I was told, 'No, this was deliberate,' and in fact they did not want the party there."

The new finance minister, and the powerful network he had around him, had already locked in the agenda. The great irony: these true believers in the contestability of markets didn't extend that view to the market for ideas.

As Shaun Goldfinch writes in his book *Remaking Australian and New Zealand Economic Policy*, the powerful personal networks of which Douglas was a part "allowed them to resist criticism, as their beliefs would receive support from the network. As key members of this network obtained senior positions throughout the bureaucracy and private sector, they were able to dominate policy formation." A crucial step was to lock in business behind the reforms: a group that had often prospered in the protected economy. A senior Treasury official, Roger Kerr, moved from the department to the New Zealand Business Roundtable. This network saw senior executives appointed to the Reserve Bank Board and brought in to run newly corporatised, then privatised, government businesses. Goldfinch notes that during the Labour and National governments between 1984 and 1999, "interest groups were often excluded from economic policy-making, influenced in part by Public Choice theory that saw them as vested interests that had contributed to economic decline, and by elitist beliefs of key politicians and policy makers." The key exception to this was the Business Roundtable. According to Lange:

> They didn't actually set the agenda but provided the taste and the appetite for it and they also provided the macho challenges ... And their mates that used to provide comment on *Morning Report* [a widely listened-to radio program] who had never made a bog in business but became business experts on Radio New Zealand.

Scale is a repeated theme in the story. In the policy and political debates around Rogernomics, it allowed a small clique to utterly dominate the shape of the economic debate.

How different was this from Australia? Many in the Australian Treasury and economics profession would have completely agreed with the thrust of what the New Zealand Treasury was telling Douglas and his government at that time. But they did not own the agenda in the same way their colleagues did in Wellington. Labor in Australia had come to office in 1983 with a very different agenda, and only found itself riding the wave of deregulation after currency speculation – and then the floating of the Australian dollar – raised inevitable internal pressures on a regulated economy.

Much was written at the time about the unprecedented power of the Treasury in Australia in the 1980s. But this power came from the political clout of its minister, Treasurer Paul Keating. The minister set the parameters of the policy, not the other way around, and he was not always in furious agreement with everything the Treasury might say.

When it came to office, the federal government was able to influence the economy through budget spending and tax, through setting interest rates and the exchange rate, and through setting wages through a centralised system. While wages were technically set by the Australian Conciliation and Arbitration Commission, the great innovation of the Hawke era was that its links with the union movement meant it could strike a deal for the wage claims made in the commission.

In an era when high inflation and industrial conflict had been running rampant, Labor was able to use its union connections to strike a wages policy designed to curb the size of wage claims and thus inflation, in exchange for commitments to other reforms and budget spending, such as the introduction of Medicare. This sort of realpolitik – being able to bend the centralised wages system into a machine to buy wage restraint – was well outside the influence, comfort zone or capabilities of Treasury officers.

This is what set the Australian and New Zealand reform experiments – and who got to shape them – apart. In both countries, players outside the parliament – notably the Treasury, Reserve Bank and business in New Zealand, and the trade unions in Australia – played significant roles. But while there was an almost unholy consensus of contested ideas in New Zealand, Australia's move to deregulate its economy was the result of intense policy debate.

Treasury was at its strongest when it was formulating tax policy but, once again, Keating set parameters where the tax reforms designed by the department, in 1985 and then in 1988, had to fit in with broader economic goals.

That's not to say that, within the bureaucracy, Treasury thinking didn't come to wield significant influence, because its officials gradually spread into other government departments, and into the burgeoning financial markets, over the following years. That entrenched a certain orthodoxy in the Australian policy debate. But this orthodoxy was also driven in part by pressures from the financial markets. Once the Australian dollar floated, it floated down in value, not up. It is hard to underestimate the impact this had on voter perceptions at the time. The world did not value Australia as highly as we did ourselves? What did we need to do to fix this? The answer, we were told by those same financial markets, was to deregulate and become more efficient and competitive.

Something else that was different in the dynamics of the political economy in the mid-1980s was that Douglas's drive to ram through massive economic reform came from a view that he would only have one term to deliver change, whereas Labor in Australia was desperately trying to establish itself as a natural party of government: that is, a government that would be in office for several terms, be regarded as a good economic manager, and be able to persuade people that they would be protected from the harshest effects of necessary change.

Hawke and Keating worked hard in the early years to earn the trust and confidence of business. Douglas didn't have quite the same problem, partly because his early push to corporatise and privatise large sections of the New Zealand economy, which until then had been run by the state, gave business a great incentive to get close to the government.

Some figures in New Zealand business would make their fortunes out of privatisation, sometimes appearing in multiple roles during the sell-off of taxpayer assets. The merchant bank Fay Richwhite & Company, for example, advised the government on the sale of 49 per cent of the Bank of New Zealand in 1989, and then purchased a third of the bank via a subsidiary.

The first wave of Rogernomics – floating the dollar, deregulating the financial markets, introducing a goods and services tax, slashing personal income tax (including halving the top rate from 66 per cent to 33 per cent), introducing a fringe benefits tax and, particularly, dumping all the subsidies and protections that sectors like agriculture had enjoyed – had already occurred when I went to New Zealand in early 1988.

Cutting spending on industry support had been at the centre of the Douglas reforms between 1984 and 1987. And it started with the sector that had been central to Australia's and New Zealand's development and wealth, and to both of our relationships with the UK: agriculture.

The extent of agricultural industry protection across the Tasman had reached truly ridiculous levels by the early 1980s. But now the country once famous for having twenty times more sheep than people showed little sentiment towards its farmers.

Subsidies had reached the point where the cost of producing agricultural goods was higher than their market price. The Lange government made them the target of the first wave of cuts. Minimum price schemes for wool, beef, sheep meat and dairy products were removed from 1984. Tax concessions and free government services for farmers went, as did land development loans, fertiliser and irrigation subsidies, and subsidised credit. Subsidies dropped from an average 24 per cent of farm incomes to just 3 per cent in five years.

The sheep flock would fall from 70 million in 1984 to 40 million in 2005. The value of farmland fell 50 per cent in real terms over four years. Many small rural towns shrunk, as people left in search of jobs elsewhere. Public services, such as schools and small hospitals, contracted.

Despite the pain these changes had caused, Labour won the 1987 election and the second wave of Rogernomics reforms got underway. Gordon Gekko had declared "Greed is good" in the movie *Wall Street*, and the great share-market crash of 1987 had prompted a global reassessment of the fashion for markets. In Australia, it unsettled the debate – at least for a few months – about the value of deregulating markets and certainly deregulating financial markets. But in New Zealand, Douglas and his allies saw the crisis as an opportunity for more reform.

Late in 1987, there was a push to have a flat tax (which was eventually dropped) and a major program of corporatising, then privatising, the huge number of government-owned businesses.

It was only at this point that Lange seemed to notice what his finance minister had got him to agree to. In January 1988, he announced it was "time for a cup of tea" and signalled that Douglas would no longer just get his own way. It was the beginning of the end of the government.

But even with restraints applied, the great sell-off got underway in earnest. The government had announced it would sell shares in state-owned businesses, including the Bank of New Zealand, New Zealand Post, Air New Zealand and the New Zealand Forestry Corporation.

The newly corporatised (and later privatised) entities slashed their workforces. The west coast of the South Island relied heavily on mining and forestry. The region suffered a 60 per cent fall in state employment between 1986 and 1991. Towns such as Reefton and Tuatapere saw an 80 per cent fall in mining jobs.

The Electricity Corporation shed 3000 jobs, the Coal Corporation 4000, New Zealand Post 8000 and, with particularly savage effects on some towns, the Forestry Corporation 5000 jobs. Within a week of the conversion of government departments into state-owned enterprises, there were close to 5000 redundancies, largely in small-town and rural New Zealand.

There had been some strange arrangements in place under Piggy Muldoon to create jobs and industry in New Zealand: televisions had to be assembled in New Zealand from imported parts, for example. But when Rogernomics swept through, towns whose economies were built on businesses like these saw their livelihood wiped out overnight.

The car assembly industry disappeared, along with a host of other industries. Job losses in the manufacturing sector were estimated to be

76,000 between 1987 and 1992. In just three years, manufacturing employment fell by 30 per cent.

It was about this time that the impact of the different sequences and priorities of reform in Australia and New Zealand became really apparent, both in their economic effects and in the way the politics played out.

Australia moved earlier on the "macro" economic changes: cuts to welfare and government capital works, rather than the subsidies being cut by the New Zealanders. The Australian government was using wages policy and tax cuts to try to curb inflation. And, crucially, the Australian economy was growing – and growing fast – through the second half of the 1980s.

By comparison, in New Zealand the rate of economic growth was starting to plummet by 1985, increasing the misery.

Australia would also see massive retrenchments in sectors that were still controlled by the government, such as electricity and telecommunications, and in sectors now exposed to competition by falling tariffs. There were huge losses in manufacturing jobs in the car and textile, clothing and footwear sectors. But these losses only really started to compound when recession hit the Australian economy in 1990–91. The "rust belt" states of Victoria and South Australia were particularly hard-hit.

The Reserve Bank of Australia later estimated that about 15 per cent of the full-time jobs lost during the recession could be attributed to the sort of "microeconomic" reforms seen in New Zealand, as opposed to the general economic downturn. But once again, these job losses tended to be concentrated in big cities, such as Melbourne and Adelaide, not spread across what was still a very large rural population in New Zealand. The effects were therefore more muted in Australia, and the visible threat of communities being wiped out by the loss of a single industry was nowhere near as great.

New Zealand moved earlier, and harder. And it also made little effort to smooth the transition for workers, and whole communities, hit by the changes. There was none of the retraining assistance, or gradual change, that Australia tried to put in place. There was none of the bargaining and trade-offs, like wage restraint in exchange for tax cuts that would help low- to middle-income earners. While Australia was introducing a universal health-care system, New Zealand would effectively get rid of its system by the early 1990s.

The radical agenda also spread much, much further. In April 1988, Roger Douglas committed the Reserve Bank of New Zealand to one of the toughest anti-inflationary policies in the world, saying he wanted inflation reduced to no more than 1 per cent a year within a couple of years. The impact of the policy on the economy – much higher real interest rates than in Australia – continued to be felt for years in the form of lower growth, even if it was not as obvious as the changes to industry policy.

At least New Zealand had an inflation target. In Australia, there was a continuing lack of clarity about whether the government or the central bank was setting interest rates. The idea was that interest rates would be set to rein in the current account deficit – that is, the gap between our imports and exports of goods and services. The government was trying to suppress the quantity of imports by keeping demand down, but also hoping investors would pour money into our productive capacity to lift the volume of exports. Using the current account deficit as a target was intended to show that the government accepted the financial markets' diagnosis that Australia was "living beyond its means." But it was a pretty useless signal when it came to setting interest rates, having little to do with what the government thought the actual cost of money should be. This would become a crucial factor in interest rates eventually rising to stratospheric levels in Australia, which helped bring on the recession in 1991.

The New Zealand economy may have had to change from the heavy regulation of the mid-1970s, given the need to stay competitive to be able to sell something to the rest of the world. And we forget so easily in Australia how expensive clothes and shoes used to be, not to mention televisions and cars, as a result of tariffs. There were similar problems in New Zealand, but more so, given relatively lower income levels. But the extent and speed of change in New Zealand, and the havoc it wreaked, would be impossible to defend from an Australian perspective. Consider, for example, the impact of the Australian recession of the early 1990s on jobs, lives and political reputations. Whatever the official figures showed about how long the economy was in recession, the worst of the recessionary conditions of record high interest rates and a collapsing job market prevailed roughly from late 1988 to 1992.

New Zealand, by comparison, experienced the longest recession of the post-war era – from 1986 to 1994 – only to go back into recession in the late 1990s. An economy that had experienced peaks of growth before the changes of as much of 4 per cent a year was suddenly lucky to manage 2 per cent – but was more often in recession for the best part of seven years.

Radical change and recession formed the backdrop to election campaigns in both Australia and New Zealand in 1990. The original authors of that radical change in New Zealand were destroyed by the internal party ructions it caused. Between the 1987 election campaign and the 1990 election, New Zealand would have three Labour prime ministers: Lange, Geoffrey Palmer and Mike Moore, who held the position for just fifty-nine days.

Palmer was thrown into the top job in August 1989, when Lange walked, eight months after a complete breakdown in relations saw Douglas out of his job. Lange's leadership had been mortally damaged by the backlash against Rogernomics among traditional Labour voters.

The party was left so broken – and broke – that it provoked an unlikely scene on election night in November 1990. Mike Moore, the short-lived prime minister who led Labour to the election, recalled the last hours in the job, shared with his wife, Yvonne, and her mother.

> As it got worse and worse, we had no money. Yvonne's mother, Yvonne and I made the sandwiches for the election-night party on Saturday night on Friday night. And we went to the party. It was a night, eh? The [diplomatic protection service] guys said the other night – actually, I'd forgotten this – "I remember when you lost the election – you were sweeping the floor out afterwards." And I said, "Yeah. So what? That's the way it is." Sweeping the floor of the hall where we had the wake.

The 1990 result was a landslide for National, led by Jim Bolger, which won 48 per cent of the vote and 69 per cent of the seats in parliament – the highest number of seats it had ever held.

National and Bolger had been elected after a campaign which had spoken of a "decent society," and with it the suggestion of a retreat from the radical and hard-edged change of Rogernomics. A shell-shocked electorate weary of reform threw out the Labour government that had visited all this upon it.

Australia, of course, had also gone to the polls in 1990, with the threat of recession hanging over the economy but not yet official, and the relationship between Hawke and Keating poisonous, but not yet fully in view of the public. The sheer dominance of the Hawke Keating team on the political stage, and their continued ability to persuade voters that while reform was hard it would bring dividends and they were the best ones to lead the country, got the government home. Australians seemed resigned to the need for change and had not yet reached the point of rejecting it.

Within hours of the New Zealand election result becoming clear, Bolger was confronted by a warning of imminent national financial collapse – just as Lange had been in 1984. This time the crisis was the fallout of the debt binge engaged in by the corporate sector in the wake of deregulation and exposed by the share-market crash of 1987.

While small-town New Zealand was enduring the pain of the sudden disappearance of subsidies and privatisation, the opening up of the financial markets and a booming share market when the Lange government came to office had seemed to give credence to the wisdom of deregulating the economy. No longer.

In Australia after the Black Monday slump of 1987, the big corporate raiders had all crashed and burned: Alan Bond, Robert Holmes à Court, John Spalvins. The same thing was happening in New Zealand. Of the top ten New Zealand corporations at the time of the '87 crash, several had been wiped out by late 1990, including companies that had briefly strode the Australian stage as raiders.

The Bank of New Zealand – which dominated the local economy – had also been taking big risks. The government had been forced into a rescue package for the bank in 1989. But no one, it seemed, realised just how much trouble it was in. "Seventeen hours after I won the election," Jim Bolger recalled, "I had officials in panic in Wellington, demanding to see me as the incoming Prime Minister that day, Sunday." The officials told the incoming prime minister that BNZ held 40 per cent of the corporate debt in New Zealand. "So if it collapsed, half of New Zealand's companies would have collapsed."

A government financial institution that had been privatised, Development Finance Corporation, also had bad debts equivalent to one-third of its loan portfolio, and the country's standing in international markets would be damaged if it was allowed to collapse.

Financial institutions in Australia – notably state banks – would also start to fail at this time, although the federal government was able to organise takeovers by other banks, rather than bailouts.

The outgoing government in New Zealand had also predicted a small budget surplus, but instead the incoming government found itself facing a deficit larger than the one later faced by Australia in the wake of the global financial crisis. This perhaps should not have been surprising, given that a global recession was hitting Australia and New Zealand hard. The smaller economy had also been savaged by exceptionally high interest rates for even longer than Australia. But the combined effect was that the party which had pledged an end to the pain, that it would pursue a "decent society," now backflipped.

Shocked to discover that it had to bail out the Bank of New Zealand and by a worse-than-expected budget position, the Bolger government turned its back on its repudiation of Rogernomics and doubled down. In the 1991 budget, in the middle of a recession, Finance Minister Ruth Richardson oversaw a savaging of the welfare budget, cutting benefits across the board, as well as introducing user-pays requirements in hospitals and schools, effectively moving from a system of free primary health care akin to

Australia's Medicare to one in which only low-income groups could get assistance. Rogernomics was replaced by "Ruthanasia."

The rents on the large stock of state-owned housing – around 70,000 houses in 1993 – were lifted from concessional to market rates, sometimes resulting in a near doubling of rent over a couple of years. A system of concessional home loans was dropped. Not surprisingly, this combination of measures hit low-income earners – who had most often been the ones to lose their jobs in the privatisation process – much harder than everyone else. It hit Māori particularly hard.

Measured inequality in New Zealand, particularly for Māori, became significantly worse. The effect was profound and long-lasting. It continues today. The number of people living in poverty shot higher. Between one in four and one in six children in New Zealand were estimated to be living in poverty in the first decades of the twenty-first century. As some commentators remarked at the time, the fiscal deficit was replaced with a social deficit.

The spending cuts from 1990 onwards were a huge drag on the economy. And the new government also blew up the industrial relations system that had been in place in New Zealand since 1894, a system broadly similar to Australia's. The country moved from laws which had been constructed in the last days of the nineteenth century to support unions, and which gave unions monopoly bargaining rights, to laws which removed all legislative support for them. It was WorkChoices on steroids.

There was no duty on employers to bargain, and no responsibility to do so in good faith. The Employment Court – replacing the old Arbitration Court – did not have the power to act if employment contracts were deemed to be "harsh" or "oppressive." The effect of the legislation in workplaces was dramatic and fast in changing the entire nature of New Zealand workplaces. Union membership halved in just five years.

New Zealand wages started to sink in real terms and relative to Australian wages, and the lure of working across the Tasman increased. Yet there has not even been a lasting rise in productivity from these changes. A recent study by the New Zealand Productivity Commission notes that workers "work longer hours for less reward than workers in most other OECD countries."

> New Zealand's labour productivity, or output per hour worked, is around 40 per cent below the average OECD benchmark. Since 1996 there has been no sign of this catching up to the top half of the OECD. Instead the gap has increased.

A range of reasons are given for this, including the small domestic market and lots of low-tech firms servicing local markets and therefore not being subjected to the pressures of a globalised market that has been transformed by technology in recent decades. But what seems certain is that radical industrial relations change has not proved any panacea.

Strangely, much of this New Zealand economic story did not make its way across the Tasman at this time. During that period of savage budgetary cuts and industrial relations change, the Coalition in Australia under John Hewson started to sell its equally hardline Fightback! package of economic reform. For a time, it seemed to prosper, particularly as the infighting between Hawke and Keating, and the savagery of recession, robbed the government of its cohesiveness and its economic management credentials.

But when Keating finally toppled Hawke after a bloody battle through 1991, he reversed the direction of policy in early 1992, promising big tax cuts and spending to kickstart the economy and isolating Hewson's push for a goods and services tax as an extra impost: a political strategy which would see Keating triumph in the 1993 election.

*

By the time of the 1993 election in New Zealand, voters there had been misled by both major parties: first by Labour, which had never mentioned its plans for dramatic reform; and then by National, which had promised to end it, then dished out even more.

The Bolger government elected just three years earlier in 1990 went from having won the largest ever majority to holding on by just one seat. The electorate savaged a government that it felt had misled it, and imposed harsh treatment on lower-income New Zealanders. But something much more important would happen at the 1993 election. And it was all the result of an accident.

As we have seen, the New Zealand political system gave Muldoon, then David Lange and Douglas, immense, and hardly checked, executive power. It was built on an unrepresentative, first-past-the-post electoral system. After two elections in 1978 and 1981 in which Labour won more votes than National, but National held on to power, there was pressure for change.

Lange's Labour established a royal commission to consider whether a proportional representation system should be introduced. But while the commission eventually recommended a mixed-member proportional (MMP) system be adopted, and that a referendum be held on the issue, there was little enthusiasm for the idea among MPs, because, as the attorney-general of the time, Geoffrey Palmer, later observed, "it was going to reduce, they thought, the power of the two major political parties."

An electoral system used with slight variations in a number of places, including Germany, Tasmania and the Australian Capital Territory, MMP involves voting for a party candidate list and a local electorate MP.

Parties are awarded a proportional share of the 120 seats in the New Zealand parliament on the basis of the number of party votes they receive. However, they must first reach one of two thresholds – by getting at least 5 per cent of the total valid party vote, or winning at least one electoral district. The result essentially is that more parties are elected to the parliament and it is much harder for a major party to govern in its own right. It usually has to form coalitions with smaller parties.

So why would any leader of a major party agree to consider this change, as Lange did during a 1987 televised leaders' debate, when he promised to hold the referendum recommended by the royal commission?

According to Palmer, Lange "thought that the [Labour Party] Policy Council had approved it, but it hadn't. He misread his briefing notes, is what happened."

To highlight that the Labour PM had gone against party policy in 1987, Opposition leader Jim Bolger promised a referendum. "Of course, after ... Bolger promised it, then the Labour Party had to change and promise it as well," Palmer recalled.

> MMP arrived: it reduced the power of the politicians and the main political parties, it was a much more democratic system, but it was not supported by either of the major political parties and it arrived because the people voted for it in a referendum. And I think that was wonderful.

Its endorsement may have been an accident, but the 54 per cent vote in favour of the new system at the 1993 referendum came at a time of intense voter disillusionment with the major parties and with radical change.

*

Having received such a resounding message from voters, the second-term Bolger government would be very different from the first. Ruth Richardson was removed from her job as finance minister as a signal to voters that the government had heeded the message. And Bolger – who is probably best described as the New Zealand equivalent of a small-l liberal – shifted his focus to other issues, most notably his commitment to Waitangi settlements, at the same time Keating was dealing with the fallout from the *Mabo* High Court decision and starting his push for Australia to become a republic.

By the time of the next Australian election in 1996, though, voters had had enough of Labor, and change, and they were offered an apparently much less frightening alternative in the form of the familiar face of John Howard, a scant policy platform and the promise that he would make voters feel "comfortable and relaxed."

That same year, New Zealand would go to its first election under the MMP system, and it revealed the continuing voter bitterness over the reform process. Minor parties sprang up. The vote splintered. Bolger was able to form a government. But a new player emerged under the MMP system: Winston Peters' New Zealand First party. Peters had been a National Party member but, opposing many of the free-market policies of both National and Labour, had established a party with a more traditional protectionist platform. The message was clear: voters wanted government at the political centre and they didn't want any more radical change. Peter's Party won 13.5 per cent of the vote and seventeen seats in the 120-seat parliament.

With these new forces at work, they were unlikely to see any. The option chosen by Howard of gaining control of the agenda – by buying control of the Senate by appointing a Labor "rat," Mal Colston, to the Senate deputy president's job – was not available to Bolger.

As was increasingly the case in the federal Coalition in Australia, National was heavy with the influence of conservatives. They grew restless with Bolger's policies and mounted a coup against him in late 1997, bringing Jenny Shipley into the job as the country's first female prime minister and a shift back to the right. That ultimately proved a disaster for National, and cleared the way for Helen Clark to lead Labour to victory in a centre-left Coalition in 1999.

And it was at this time, as we were about to enter the new century, that the paths of our two countries, in the way we went about change, politics and national debate, started to diverge wildly.

Helen Clark would be the first prime minister in New Zealand in fifteen years who did not come into office and immediately repudiate everything she had pledged on the way there. And she was also the first to acknowledge that the costs of change had been too high.

The traumatic times instituted by her own party – and a government of which she was a part – were a "ghastly period," she would later say. The issue of trust was "a huge preoccupation for me" while campaigning:

> People [had] voted for Labour, they didn't expect what they got. They voted for National in 1990 … they didn't expect what they got. There was no signalling of huge welfare cuts and all the stuff that happened … So trust was extremely low. No one believed anything anybody said. And you had to be very clear – "This is what I'm gonna do and this is what I'm going to stick to" – to rebuild trust in politics.

Unlike Lange and Bolger, Clark was not compelled to undertake even more radical reform: the national economy had finally started to pick up in the mid-1990s after almost a decade of recessionary conditions. The budget was in surplus.

Her government would become better known over time for social change, reorienting foreign policy and undoing some of the economic changes of earlier governments.

She was leading a coalition government which reflected the bitter split in her own party as a result of Rogernomics: she relied on the support of a new minor party, the Alliance Party, led by a former Labour MP, Jim Anderton, and, like Bolger before her, on Peters' New Zealand First.

The split between the politics of New Zealand and Australia was underway. It was Howard who started what have become known as the "culture wars" in Australia. Even before he was elected in 1996, he had railed against political "elites," who he claimed had captured the Labor government and the political debate during its time in office. This included everyone from Aboriginal people to those in the performing arts, the welfare "lobby" to multicultural Australia. He promised to govern "for all of us," in an appeal to average Australians who felt they had been excluded from political favours, but sacrificed on the altar of economic change.

Somehow – a bit like the Business Roundtable in New Zealand fifteen years earlier – the idea of vested interests having a bad impact on policy-making did not extend to the business world in Australia. Having come to office with a relatively limited agenda, Howard succumbed to business pressure to look like he was "doing something" on reform in 1997 and set in train the process that would eventually lead to tax reforms, including the introduction of a goods and services tax.

Across the Tasman, on the other hand, Clark wound back the more radical elements of National's industrial relations changes, set up a new savings bank, Kiwibank, based in the post office (replacing one that had been sold off to ANZ), and renationalised Air New Zealand after the airline's disastrous takeover bid for Ansett. The government gradually bought back the national railway system. She would remove the right of appeal to the Privy Council in London and establish a Supreme Court, legalise civil unions and decriminalise sex work.

The powerful network that had backed the Rogernomics agenda had not gone away, and was not happy: the new government faced a year-long public assault on its competence and policies. Clark recalled later: "They were very, very aggressive. Fundamentally, they didn't like the 1999 election result. Probably didn't like the other election results where we won much more either. So they dug in."

It became known as the Winter of Discontent. Roger Kerr, at the Business Roundtable, called the new government's policies "radical" and "Muldoonist." Economists said the government had no idea about running a business and that it was tarred with a "socialist mentality" that repelled overseas investment. *The Australian Financial Review* warned that New Zealand would be economically isolated and perceived as having "lost the plot."

But where Clark really started to make an international mark was in foreign policy. If you asked many Australians what they knew of how New Zealand had conducted its foreign policy in recent decades, they would quite likely hark back to the 1980s and the Lange government's stance against the visit of ships from the US Navy that might carry nuclear weapons. It put the country – and its government – on the world stage. The tiny upstart was thumbing its nose at its mighty alliance partner, and in the process, it seemed in Australia, at us too. It was the event which created the biggest sense of separation between the two countries.

Lange won government in 1984 in an election prompted by an argument over legislation to make New Zealand nuclear-free. He had campaigned hard on the issue, including against visits by American nuclear ships. Since the United States had a "neither confirm nor deny" policy about the nuclear status of its vessels, this would inevitably lead to a clash with the Americans.

New Zealand, along with Australia and most South Pacific nations, also signed a treaty in 1985 declaring the South Pacific a nuclear-free zone, which made their hostility to French testing explicit. And it was this part of New Zealand's anti-nuclear policy that would crystallise the country's position in Lange's mind.

French agents bombed the *Rainbow Warrior* – a Greenpeace protest vessel that campaigned against nuclear testing – in Auckland Harbour in July 1985, resulting in the drowning of a photographer on board.

"The *Rainbow Warrior* was the defining moment for me because I knew it was the end of any New Zealand commitment to the so-called Western Alliance," Lange said in 1996.

> It was not when it was sunk … but when we knew who had sunk it that I knew. And then the overwhelming silence from Great Britain. I mean, Margaret Thatcher was prepared to condemn Gaddafi for everything, but the French could go and kill people in our harbour. Hawke never said a word. Ronald Reagan pretended total indifference. We never heard a peep out of those people who we

were allegedly in a Western alliance with ... those people we fought with for democracy.

The decision to ban US nuclear ships from visiting New Zealand ports saw it frozen out of the ANZUS security alliance with the United States and Australia. Lange said that if this was the price New Zealand must pay to remain nuclear-free, "it is the price we are prepared to pay." The majority of New Zealanders backed the trade-off, and National came to support the position too.

Helen Clark had been a key figure within Labour ranks who had kept up the pressure on Lange on anti-nuclear and disarmament issues.

New Zealanders came to be very proud of the country's independent foreign policy from the 1980s. It came to be part of its brand in the world, a cultural value almost. Some insiders observe that it has involved costs: the absence of a free trade agreement with the United States, for example; an overinvestment in multinational deployments around the world "to maintain a sense of usefulness"; and, in more recent times, diplomats having to put in considerable effort to make clear New Zealand couldn't be peeled away – by China – from the countries with which it had traditionally been close, no matter how much it was taking a more independent line. The government was forced to put a lot more money into information collection services, including satellites, and into lifting the quality of its intelligence agencies.

Publicly, the country chose a path for itself, and an international identity, built on championing multilateral organisations, such as the United Nations, and multinational peacekeeping forces. It built up its presence and understanding of the Pacific, brokering peace talks in Bougainville in 1997 that would help to end the bloody civil war in Papua New Guinea.

The relationship with Australia remained cordial but just a little distant. Don McKinnon, New Zealand's foreign minister from 1990 to 1999, captures the prevalent mood when Howard came to office in 1996. Howard made it clear, McKinnon says, that "he could work with us, but recognised the differences." It is not dissimilar language in its stiff politeness to that used about much more distant countries.

New Zealand's stance in the world would alter after the attacks on the World Trade Center in New York and the Pentagon in September 2001. The relationship with the United States improved under Clark as a result of New Zealand's commitment to support the war in Afghanistan – although, as we saw at the beginning of the essay, Clark would not join the Coalition of the Willing in Iraq in 2003. She tells me New Zealanders "really don't like our troops being deployed much" – and indeed even the limited deployment to Afghanistan split her coalition with Anderton's Alliance Party.

The backdrop to the political discussion about Afghanistan and Iraq was also very different in New Zealand to the one we were having in Australia. National security and the threat of terrorism did not become one of the framing features of politics, or policy obsessions, as it did in Australia under Howard after 9/11. Clark says the events of September 2001 "seemed a long way away. People didn't see them as something that would happen here."

Of course, in Australia the politics of national security and terrorism were also very much bound up with the issue of asylum seekers. To many Australians who did not approve of Howard's refusal, in August 2001, to let the container ship MV *Tampa* – carrying hundreds of refugees – enter Australian waters, New Zealand became a symbol of the right way to treat refugees. That view has largely continued with the standing offer by New Zealand to take some of the asylum seekers stuck for years in our offshore detention system.

It is worth quoting Clark at length on this, as it reflects the more pragmatic realities of New Zealand's position. She told journalist Guyon Espiner in 2016 that as the *Tampa* crisis unfolded, the New Zealand media started to ask what the government would do if it faced the same circumstances as Australia. She responded that she assumed "we would escort the vessel into port and process people according to international conventions on refugees and asylum seekers." This prompted a phone call from Australian foreign minister Alexander Downer asking if New Zealand could help.

Immigration was very worried about it because they said it would set a precedent for boats coming here. I said, "What boat has ever come here, since our forebears came on sailing ships?" I mean, we are so remote. From time to time there's been scares about boats coming. They never come. It's too far. So there was hardly a precedent. The greatest number of asylum seekers we'd ever had was twelve on one plane, and that stopped as well, when we began the advance passenger processing post-9/11. So I didn't think we were in any great danger of attracting boats of asylum seekers by doing something humane for the *Tampa* people. So, eventually, we made the decision that we would offer to take all of the family groups and the children under eighteen.

While there was initially a backlash, "when the decision was made and the reasons were set out, public opinion did change, quite significantly. And over time I think one of the really nice things about New Zealand is that people took the Afghan refugees, particularly the minors, to their hearts and followed the stories of what happened with these boys."

Having thawed the relationship with the United States, Clark was able to continue to build New Zealand's reputation as a multilateralist, but one not linked to the US, as Australia was perceived to be.

Despite the national pride in pursuing an independent path despite its small size, there is a pragmatic truth that lies underneath New Zealand's position: the country relies on an assumption that it is not really a target for invasion and, more significantly, that it can free-ride on Australia's defence capabilities if it were ever to get into trouble.

Reviewing the defence spending of the two countries in 2018, Australian Strategic Policy Institute analyst Mark Thomson noted that:

Although both countries share the goal of peace and security in a rules-based world, they pursue that goal with very different intensities. Australia systematically accepts higher costs and risks than New Zealand does. New Zealanders each contribute NZ$426 to their defence; Australians spend A$1438.

New Zealand doesn't match Australia's effort because it knows that Australia will shoulder the burden, at least in the local region. In exactly the same way, Australia relies on the US to shoulder the burden in the broader region. Lest there be any doubt of the pattern of reliance down the alliance chain, in recent times the US has spent around twice the share of its GDP on defence as has Australia, and Australia has spent more than twice the share as has New Zealand.

So New Zealand has been largely free of a defence budget proportional to Australia's, and also of the massive national security apparatus constructed in Australia after 9/11.

*

Aiding the nation's finances was the fact that, by the early 2000s, the transformation had begun to an economy that made much of its money from dairy and tourism. The Lord of the Rings trilogy was filmed during 1999 and 2000, and the films would go on to support a tourism industry in their own right.

But the expansion of dairy and tourism pointed to a major conflict in New Zealand's economy that would also help reframe the political debate. The shape of New Zealand agriculture was changing because of declining prices for sheep and beef. With only wine and some horticulture as alternative international growth markets, New Zealand turned to dairy as its agricultural trade saviour. Land was becoming available to dairy as less profitable sectors declined. New Zealand restructured and created what is for all intents and purposes a monopoly processor which now strides the world on a grand scale, a "national champion": Fonterra.

The sheer scale of Fonterra in the New Zealand economy – and in the global milk market – is extraordinary. It is the processor for around 90 per cent of New Zealand's dairy farmers. By the mid-2000s it was the world's largest processor of raw milk and one of the top ten dairy companies in the world. It has at times contributed about one-quarter of New Zealand's export earnings and 7 per cent of the country's GDP (a performance that is strikingly different to the struggles our own dairy industry has faced in the wake of deregulation).

The NZ industry was able to capitalise on big shifts in global markets, and also enjoyed some luck, most notably the exponential growth in Chinese demand, particularly for milk powder and baby formula. Between 2008 and 2013, imports of whole milk powder to China increased more than sixfold, with 91 per cent imported from New Zealand.

But there have been significant costs to New Zealand's dairy success. The massive expansion of the industry has polluted New Zealand's rivers, and the sparse, arid but mountainous beauty of the South Island started to be afflicted by lurid green circles of highly fertilised and irrigated land for dairy cattle. And cows fart: a lot.

New Zealand was building a "clean and green" image, like the one promoted by Tasmania. It was the basis of everything from its competitive advantage in food exports to part of its attraction as a tourist destination. So the contamination issues posed a very real and conspicuous threat to the economy, let alone the environment.

Unlike the government in Australia, Clark's government signed up to the Kyoto Protocol in 2002, in the face of resistance from the Opposition, business and farmers. New Zealand committed to reduce greenhouse gases to 1990 levels in a process that would start in 2008. For New Zealand, the problem was going to be the agriculture sector, just as the coal industry was for Australia. Methane is actually a much more potent greenhouse gas than carbon dioxide – about twenty-eight times more dangerous. In a refrain all too familiar in Australia, the charge was that adopting these targets would damage the country's international competitiveness.

In 2007, Clark unveiled New Zealand's version of an emissions trading scheme, at the very time shifting opinion in Australia prompted Howard to embrace the idea. Right from the start, the New Zealand scheme had significant flaws. Most conspicuously, it didn't include the most contentious area of emissions – agriculture – in any substantive way, mostly because of the (ongoing) problem of measuring methane gas emissions from cows and doing anything about them. But it was also a "cap and trade" system, without any firm cap on the actual amount of emissions produced.

The efficacy of the scheme has never been very great. Even in a country with 80 per cent renewable energy from hydroelectricity, and which managed to legislate an ETS, doing something about climate change remains more aspiration than policy. But while the nature of the scheme may have been disputed and contentious, there has not been the sort of debate we have seen in Australia, which went back to challenging the very science of climate change and dismantling policies to deal with it.

By this time, both Clark's government, and Howard's, were seriously ageing institutions. Howard's resistance to doing something about climate change would be one of several issues that a new Labor leader in Australia, Kevin Rudd, would capitalise on in the 2007 election, pledging to bring real change to Australia's policies

Almost a year later, Clark would also have to go to the polls. But climate change was not the hot issue it was in Australia, mostly because New Zealand was back in a domestic recession, and was about to be engulfed – along with the rest of the world – by the GFC. The economy would dominate all in the election.

The dynamics of the 2008 election campaign were set by the arrival in 2006 of a personable and credible leader of the National Party, a former banker named John Key.

While New Zealand had gone through a long period of growth under Clark's Labour, the government was perceived by some as a "do-nothing" economic manager. Key found a palpable symbol for the sense that the country was floundering: the "Brain Drain." This had been a real thing in New Zealand for some decades: certainly as far back as the time Piggy Muldoon made a famous joke about New Zealand migration to Australia boosting the IQ of both countries. But by now, income per person had fallen around 35 per cent behind the Australian level.

Key raised the simple question of why everyone kept leaving. National put billboards up around the country's big cities: "Wave goodbye to higher taxes, not your loved ones."

In Australia, budget surpluses built on the biggest resources boom in our history had seen tax cuts become an almost annual event through the first decade of the twenty-first century. But Clark and her finance minister, Michael Cullen, had resisted pressure for tax cuts for much of their time in office, as the economy continued to grow and the budget bottom line improved. And New Zealand did not have the manna of Australia's resources boom.

The New Zealand central bank's tough anti-inflation policies were keeping interest rates high as the country headed towards the polls. Fuel and food prices were high too, and the economy slipped into recession in early 2008. The conditions were perfect for a former banker to capitalise on growing disillusionment with Labour's economic management and run on a platform which promised superior economic knowhow and policy can-do.

Like every government since 1990, Key's political message was one of the centre, not the radical right or of radical change. And Key added optimism: something in short supply when the global trainwreck of the GFC hit in the middle of the New Zealand election campaign.

Kiwis went to the polls on 8 November, five days after Barack Obama was elected in the US. National won 45 per cent of the party vote and 59 per cent of the 122 seats in parliament. It did not go into a formal Coalition, but governed as a minority government with guarantees from a number of parties.

Australia and New Zealand had flipped their political allegiances once more, with Australia re-embracing Labor, and New Zealand moving back to the free-market National Party. But they also diverged spectacularly in their response to the GFC. The Key government's budget response was almost undetectable compared to the Rudd government's two stimulus packages. And the new government had the backing of the New Zealand Treasury to not do very much, in stark comparison with the Australian Treasury's famous advice to "go early, go hard, go households."

Even though Key had stuck to the centre of politics in his campaigning, the position his finance minister took on the causes and cures of the crisis was staggeringly hardline. Key's minister, Bill English, framed the GFC as one caused by "Labour's complacency and refusal to address structural issues dragging down our growth potential," rather than the result of one of the biggest-ever shocks to the global financial system. He was pushing the case for more free-market reforms at the very time Australian prime minister Kevin Rudd was proclaiming the GFC as the death of neoliberalism.

Business New Zealand had even argued in the week before the election for a classic "neoliberal" response to the crisis. "It is not, as claimed by some, a failure of markets or a failure of capitalism," the lobby group said.

> Instead, it was interventions by governments and central banks – promoting the expansion of too-easy credit and underwriting mortgage and other schemes without sufficient asset backing – that caused the debacle. The lesson to be drawn is not that there is something at fault within markets, but that governments can cause huge problems by intervening in markets.

The Kiwi economy – already in recession when the GFC hit – stayed that way until late 2009, when the massive fiscal stimulus put in place by

China, and then Australia, helped gradually push the New Zealand economy back into furtive growth.

New Zealand remained a relatively tiny cork floating in the global economic sea, and the GFC confirmed its vulnerability to these forces was even greater than Australia's.

But whatever the huge differences in the two countries' attempts to deal with fallout of the GFC, they faced a curiously similar problem in 2009 and 2010, which reflected another aspect of their vulnerability to powerful global interests. In Australia, an overly ambitious attempt to rethink the entire tax system would eventually bring the weight of the business sector, and the conservative establishment, down on the Rudd government with unprecedented aggression. The debate about a proposed resources rent tax was at the heart of the battle which would eventually topple a prime minister. It revealed the power and willingness of the international mining industry to threaten a sovereign government over policy.

If there was an equivalent showdown in New Zealand, it concerned the unlikely subject of hobbits. The Lord of the Rings franchise had also made New Zealand, and particularly Wellington, a hub for all the skills involved in making high-tech movies.

However, even maintaining the base conditions under which people were expected to work was becoming fraught in the first years of the new century. There had been a gradual erosion of employment terms, covering things like the postponement of a project, overtime and time off. Lacking bargaining muscle, the union judged it would need the support of international performers to enforce base rates, and waited for a major production which would involve performers who were used to striking collective bargains everywhere else in the world.

That opportunity came when the New Zealand director of the Lord of the Rings series, Peter Jackson, and Warner Bros. turned their attention to new movies based on J.R.R. Tolkien's The Hobbit. Crucial to what would happen next was the employment status of workers in the industry: were they contractors or employees? (The same issue would later bedevil the arts in Australia during the pandemic, when they were largely denied JobKeeper support because they were not "employees.")

In May 2010, Warner Bros. circulated contracts which made clear it would not hire workers for the *Hobbit* series on collectively bargained contracts. The International Federation of Actors responded by advising the producers that until there had been a meeting with the Media Entertainment and Arts Alliance (the Australian union which was seeking to assist its Kiwi counterpart), it would be advising its members not to sign any contracts. In reply, Jackson threatened to take the filming of the movies – and all production – to Eastern Europe, portraying the dispute as a case of an "Australian bully boy" (that is, the MEAA) pursuing an agenda "based on money and power." Jackson released a long statement, saying, "it feels as if we have a large Aussie cousin kicking sand in our eyes ... or to put it another way, opportunists exploiting our film for their own political gain ... If *The Hobbit* goes east – Eastern Europe in fact – look forward to a long, dry big-budget movie drought in this country."

It is here the story gets a little darker, amid growing alarm in New Zealand about the economic impact of losing international film productions. A solution seemed to be in sight after a meeting in October, but Jackson and his partner, Fran Walsh, then released a statement saying that Warner Bros. executives would be "coming down to New Zealand to make arrangements to move the production offshore."

The dispute became very bitter. There were rallies around the country. Actors' representatives received death threats and were abused in public. Reuters reported on 25 October that "thousands of New Zealanders" had taken to the streets that day "to protest against possible plans to move production of Peter Jackson's 'Hobbit' movies overseas."

> With some dressed as hobbits or other characters from Middle Earth, they carried banners saying "New Zealand is Middle Earth" and "We love Hobbits," aiming to reassure nervous Hollywood studio executives rattled by a short-lived union boycott. The rallies were held

a day before representatives from Warner Bros. Pictures were due to arrive in New Zealand to decide where to shoot the lucrative $500 million adaptation of the J.R.R. Tolkien fantasy.

Warners executives were rushed straight off the plane to negotiate with the prime minister. Two days later, Key announced an agreement had been reached with the company that the films would be made in New Zealand, in return for special industrial laws and an increased payout to the film company. On top of the standard 15 per cent tax break for film producers, there would be US$7.5 million for each movie. The government even agreed to pay US$10 million towards marketing the movies.

The New York Times reported that:

> behind the agreement is a hard economic reality. Hollywood has the upper hand in deciding where to film its big-budget extravaganzas, and there are many places willing to pay to attract filmmakers.
>
> And so the negotiations found executives of a giant American studio sitting across the table from the chief executive of a sovereign nation, population 4.4 million, wrangling over the fate of a pair of films and, with it, a not insignificant part of that nation's economy and public image.

In an editorial headed "Price to keep *Hobbit* in NZ is extortionate," the *New Zealand Herald* wrote on 29 October that "at some point during the negotiations over *The Hobbit*, someone should have stepped back and asked how much it was actually worth to this country to keep the filming here," since the result had been "for New Zealand to jettison part of its workplace law and compromise its economic principles."

The government rushed legislation through parliament within twenty-four hours that removed the right of any film worker to challenge their employment status, or to collectively bargain. The legislation was in breach of international labour conventions.

Hearing the story of the *Hobbit* dispute, it was hard not to think of the mining-tax brawl in Australia that same year. As part of the makeover of government policy when she became prime minister, Julia Gillard vowed to end the mining industry's attack on the government over a super-profits tax.

An enduring image of that episode was of food being wheeled in on trolleys to the cabinet room in Parliament House, where mining company executives were essentially writing a new version of the tax. Originally forecast to raise about $6 billion a year in the 2012–13 budget, the tax likely collected as little as $200 million in 2013–14. A couple of years later, the government stopped including a separate number for the tax in the budget papers at all, citing taxpayer confidentiality.

*

After the *Hobbit* dispute, New Zealand was shaken by a more existential threat. The earthquake that hit Christchurch at lunchtime on 22 February 2011 killed 181 people and destroyed about a third of the buildings in the city's central business district. Large swathes of the CBD have not been rebuilt ten years later.

The task of rebuilding the city, however, also represented a massive stimulus to the national economy. Combined with a surge in demand from China, higher export prices and accelerating tourism, growth took off between 2010 and 2015. After years of economic hardship and volatility, there was finally a more solid sense of prosperity in the country.

Australia had weathered the economic fallout of the GFC much better than New Zealand but had entered a new era of ruthless politics and insta-bility. Suddenly it was Australia that was the land of minority governments and uncertainty. New Zealand under Key was feeling confident. During his time in office, the Kiwi prime minister would deal with four Australian prime ministers but came within just one seat of being the first PM of the MMP era to win government in his own right.

New Zealanders started to come home, prodding the economy along even faster. Emigration had become a huge swing factor in the New Zealand economy, compared to Australia, which had enjoyed much higher and more consistent migration growth while the two economies had been undergoing their transformations.

A constant drain of people had – and has – knock-on economic effects. Consider, for example, how the Australian economy has been geared to the confident presumption of a growing population. The housing industry has come to be organised for mass-produced housing divisions and, more recently, apartment blocks to cope with all the extra people who arrive each year.

The situation was very different in New Zealand. Its housing industry is still not equipped to build at scale after years of variable population growth. The Brain Drain to Australia partially comprised a tradie drain. Housing costs in New Zealand are much higher. Individual, bespoke houses still predominate.

Housing prices escalated, particularly in Auckland. This led to resentment about the sale of land to foreigners. These housing pressures, along with the underlying rise in inequality that dated back to the 1980s and 1990s, started to emerge as issues at the 2014 election. But Key's popularity was at its zenith and the country was feeling confident. The influx of people may have been a problem, but from 2015 it was contributing around half of New Zealand's annual economic growth, meaning that for the first time in recent memory the drivers of the New Zealand economy looked a little like Australia's.

Underlying the prosperity of both countries, of course, was China. And there was no developed country in the world that seemed to hitch its star to the rising superpower quite so enthusiastically as New Zealand.

CHINA

When National prime minister John Key and his government were elected in 2008, the country had taken on a businessman who was late to politics – not unlike Australia's Malcolm Turnbull – and who had a particularly pragmatic view of how his country's relationship with China would develop.

A relationship with the United States that had developed a distinct chill over nuclear ships in the Lange era had thawed under Clark as a result of New Zealand's participation in the war in Afghanistan. Key oversaw New Zealand being formally brought in from the cold with the signing of the Wellington Declaration in 2010, a strategic partnership covering issues from nuclear proliferation to climate change. He also had a warm personal relationship with US president Barack Obama.

But Key's focus was a trade relationship with China. New Zealand was the first developed country to sign a free trade agreement with China, in 2008, some seven years before Australia. This was one of a number of firsts New Zealand scored with the new economic superpower: in 1997, it became the first developed country to agree to China's accession to the World Trade Organization; in 2004, it was the first developed country to recognise China as a market economy.

Strategically, the New Zealanders believed the history of their relationship with the United States, and their subsequent projection of themselves as independent multilateralists, gave them a unique position. "Our perceived independence meant we felt we could be an honest broker," one official told me. "We'd go to both places and they'd ask about the other, whereas Australia was a bit different. It was seen as part of the US camp."

New Zealand officials believe they played a key role in getting support for the Trans-Pacific Partnership from the Democrats in America by selling the geopolitical significance of the deal. And New Zealand, along with Australia, pushed the "pivot" by the Obama administration to Asia and the Pacific (though that amounted to little).

The Kiwi approach to China stood in marked contrast to the more hawkish view taken by Australia's new prime minister, Kevin Rudd. The 2009 defence white paper squarely addressed Chinese military expansion, amid rising concern about a wavering commitment of the United States to the Asia-Pacific, noting that "the pace, scope and structure of China's military modernisation ha[s] the potential to give its neighbours cause for concern if not carefully explained, and if China does not reach out to others to build confidence regarding its military plans."

To outrage from Beijing, the Australian government also put tougher foreign investment curbs on Chinese state-owned enterprises, a move not pursued in New Zealand.

Analyst Patrick Köllner notes that, by comparison, the New Zealand white paper:

> took a fairly benign view of the security implications of China's rise, noting that the PRC "both benefit[ed] from and contribute[d] to regional stability and prosperity" and that there was "a natural tendency for it to define and pursue its interests in a more forthright way on the back of growing wealth and power."

New Zealand's approach to China was beginning to cause alarm in Australia and the United States.

Australia, Canada, New Zealand, the United Kingdom and the United States are parties to a treaty for joint cooperation in signals intelligence known as the Five Eyes. Following New Zealand's refusal to welcome US nuclear-armed naval vessels, the public posturing of the former ANZUS alliance partners – the US, Australia and New Zealand – had clearly left New Zealand out in the cold. But the reality was that New Zealand kept its connections with the United States and Australia, along with a number of Western allies, as a member of the intelligence alliance. Its geographical location meant it provided a crucial time window around the globe into what has become an increasingly sophisticated global intelligence listening operation. In the words of one Australian security figure, New Zealand was Five Eyes' "night watchman."

Don McKinnon says New Zealand also used its preparedness and usefulness in multilateral operations to gradually win back much of the US intelligence it lost after the nuclear ships decision. For example, in responding to a US request to provide troops for Haiti, and later Somalia and Bosnia-Herzegovina, the argument was put that it was hard to deploy troops to these places when New Zealand had been chopped out of receiving intelligence about them. So New Zealand was able to make the most of its public image as the assertive minnow on the world stage, while still keeping ties with Western allies which made it valuable.

There were some important knock-on effects at home from its foreign policy positions. The country seemed to be spared a lot of the angst Australia went through in the 1980s and '90s – and beyond – about its relationship with Asia (was it part of it or not?) and about choosing between the United States and China.

Even so, by the time Tony Abbott became prime minister in 2013, there was concern that New Zealand was not pulling its weight in the Five Eyes: that its intelligence budget was focused purely domestically; that it had pulled back from the Pacific. Indeed, it was increasingly referred to as the "soft underbelly" of the alliance.

When Abbott met with Key, the subject of New Zealand's investment in Five Eyes came up. Abbott responded to Key's remarks about Five Eyes by observing that the alliance was "more four eyes and a blink." A rocked Key responded by offering to expand New Zealand's listening posts in the South Pacific.

Like Turnbull, Key had done business in China and started his prime ministership with that sense of the emerging economic giant. "He never looked at China through any prism other than as a businessman," one New Zealand official says.

But while Turnbull came to be persuaded by intelligence agencies and advisers of the growing strategic problems China represented, New Zealand continued to see it primarily as a trade partner, and took what Canberra and Washington believed to be a too-benign view of its intentions.

New Zealand's relationship with China developed further: it became the first developed country to become a prospective founding member of the China-led Asian Infrastructure Investment Bank. There were negotiations to upgrade the FTA, and in April 2017 the two countries signed a "Memorandum of Arrangement on Strengthening Cooperation on China's Belt and Road Initiative."

The Belt and Road Initiative is the massive push by China to build sea and land links through the purchase of ports and infrastructure investments in a host of nations, including relatively poor countries in the Pacific. Australia remained dubious about the BRI and China's potential use of it to get a strategic foothold around the world. But New Zealand authorities, according to Köllner, "decided to be at the table, to try to shape the Initiative in areas where it touches on New Zealand interests, such as the Pacific."

By now Australia and New Zealand had very different approaches – and politics – when it came to national security and intelligence. These issues had become an almost obsessive focus in Australia in the wake of the terror attacks of 2001. Australia increasingly sent out warning signals across the Tasman, particularly concerned about the BRI, which saw the Chinese invest in areas New Zealand regarded as within its sphere of influence: Polynesia, Samoa, even the Cook Islands. There were also concerns about Wellington's reluctance to criticise Beijing over incursions in the South China Sea.

New Zealand's noted China scholar Anne-Marie Brady summed up the concerns when she wrote in late 2018 about why New Zealand was of such interest to China. There was its responsibility for the defence and foreign policy of three other territories: the Cook Islands, Niue and Tokelau, potentially meaning four votes for China at international organisations. There were its links into the South Pacific, as well as its status as a claimant state in Antarctica, where the Chinese government has a long-term strategic agenda.

New Zealand's cheap arable land and sparse population was attractive to a country seeking to improve its food security. And then there was the Five Eyes alliance. Brady wrote:

Extricating New Zealand from these military groupings and away from its traditional partners, or at least getting New Zealand to agree to stop spying on the PRC for the Five Eyes, would be a major coup for the Xi Government's strategic goal of turning China into a global great power.

New Zealand's economic, political, and military relationship with China is seen by Beijing as a model to Australia, the small island nations in the South Pacific, and more broadly, other Western states. New Zealand is also a potential strategic site for the PLA Navy's Southern Hemisphere naval facilities and a future Beidou ground station – there are already several of these in Antarctica. All of these reasons make New Zealand of considerable interest to China under Xi Jinping.

Concern about Chinese attempts to infiltrate and influence New Zealand domestic politics erupted at the same time it became a major issue in Australia in the controversy over NSW Labor senator Sam Dastyari. In 2017, it emerged that a long-serving New Zealand National MP, Yang Jian, had worked for a Chinese military intelligence school for a number of years and was a member of the Chinese Communist Party, but had failed to mention these facts when applying for residency, citizenship and jobs. The Asia editor of the *Financial Times*, Jamil Anderlini, noted afterwards that "some of the biggest donors to the main political parties [in New Zealand] are China-based businessmen with close ties to the Communist party."

> Campaign finance legislation rushed through parliament last month has done little to close off the loopholes that allow this kind of influence-buying. Astonishingly, a man who spent at least 15 years working for China's military intelligence apparatus remains an elected member of parliament, even after admitting he was ordered by the party to conceal his past on his New Zealand immigration application.

Anderlini wrote that a "senior intelligence official from one of [the Five Eyes] countries spoke of New Zealand's 'supine' attitude to China and its 'compromised political system.'"

Australian officials believe their New Zealand counterparts have belatedly come to see the less benign side of the relationship with China. But the small country is much more economically exposed to the new superpower, both because of its exports and because its largest proportion of international students comes from China. Brady wrote in July 2020 that, since 2017:

> the New Zealand government has attempted to make a calculated correction … [But it] has strenuously avoided confronting China directly. Instead, since coming to power in 2017, the Labor–New Zealand First–Greens Coalition government has carefully managed a case-by-case recalibration of the New Zealand–China relationship, all the while claiming any changes were "country agnostic." Unlike the prime ministers of Australia and the UK, New Zealand Prime Minister Jacinda Ardern avoided New Zealand's China risk-mitigation policies being associated with herself, or any one minister. Each new policy initiative has been debated publicly and then, if approved, backed up with legislation. As with the previous National-led government, any policy decisions that affected China, such as … the ban on Huawei in 5G, were described as following a proper process, responding to legislative requirements. The COVID-19 pandemic has deepened this quiet recalibration.

I ask the prime minister who had overseen the signing of the free trade deal with China in 2008, Helen Clark, to reflect on how things have developed. "My view is that the question is not whether you engage with China, but how," she says. "Kevin Rudd had sensible things to say about this: that a megaphone doesn't work, that you have to work pragmatically."

The free trade deal was a huge boon for New Zealand, she says, but she is adamant that there has been "enormous naivety" in what has followed since. "It has been too easy for government, trade officials and the business community to think that, having scored the deal, there was no need to bother with other countries. We became too dependent." There has been a recent attempt to rebalance trade with Japan, Europe and Korea.

What of China's more assertive approach in the Pacific – the region where New Zealand feels it has a special relationship? Clearly, Australia and New Zealand can't outspend China. So that means we have to be in relationships more than partnerships, and deliver things that are more useful than just new parliamentary buildings – providing services such as health care, and access to education systems, skills training and work opportunities.

The rise of China poses challenges to a really small country with a history so like Australia's in many ways. New Zealand's determination not to join the Australian federation and its competitive rivalry with Australia for Britain's affection in the early years of the twentieth century was replaced by a proud assertion of independence from the new global superpower – the United States – in the late twentieth century, after it was abandoned by Britain. But there is now a growing unease in New Zealand that it is once more at the mercy of a global superpower, at least economically.

Australia, with what the eminent foreign policy adviser Allan Gyngell has described as its longstanding "fear of abandonment," has, by contrast, moved from a close commitment to Britain to an equally great psychological and strategic dependence on the United States.

China now looms not only as an economic superpower over both economies, but as the new bully on the block: a bully that doesn't just represent a large chunk of our export markets, but one that in the past five years has thrown its weight around in the region, and even within our own countries. This has provoked very different responses from Australia and New Zealand, and as a result has created tensions between our two countries.

We have travelled quite different paths in foreign and defence policy in the half-century since we were set adrift by the UK.

A global pandemic changed the rules of politics around the world in 2020, seeming to make all previous rules redundant. Political controversies and domestic political spats could be brushed aside with assertion of the need for a statesmanlike focus on the crisis at hand. There was more tolerance for governments exercising executive power, and for governments committing eye-watering amounts of money to the health system and to propping up their nation's economy. Oppositions seemed to fade into irrelevance.

The pandemic established whole new agendas, or revived neglected ones. Why on earth hadn't anyone paid proper attention to the shocking state of aged care? How had the conditions in our workforce become so compromised that casualisation now posed a health risk to us all? How would our economies prosper without the stimulus of relentless population growth?

In countries facing elections in the middle of this, the sole issue seemed to be the virus and how their leaders were dealing with it. In the United States, the focus was Trump. The president's shambolic handling of COVID-19 seemed to be the only thing that raised real questions about his re-election through much of 2020, pushing him into the last refuge of the scoundrel: a campaign ostensibly based on law and order, and the balance of the Supreme Court, but in truth pitting American communities against each other.

New Zealand was also going to the polls as the pandemic raged almost everywhere in the world – except in New Zealand. When Labour, which had been in coalition government since October 2017, released its first 2020 election campaign ad, there was just one image and one message: Jacinda Ardern and her leadership.

The prime minister sat at a desk, speaking straight down the camera to voters. "Together we went hard and early to fight COVID," she said. "Our plan now is to build the economy even stronger." There were general references to creating jobs and backing business, but it was really about faith in Ardern's leadership. "We can see what we can do with a plan," she said.

The prime minister was up against her third Opposition leader in four months. The National Party floundered in the wake of the government's success, not just in tackling the virus, but in getting the domestic economy moving again. In July 2020, National had chosen the tough veteran MP Judith Collins to take on Ardern. Known as "Crusher Collins" from her days when, as a minister in the Key government, she had advocated crushing the cars of boy street racers, Collins represented a shift back to a more hardline economic conservatism. But it was hard to find space for difference. After all, one of her two predecessors in 2020, Simon Bridges, had been toppled in a run of events that started when he had put up some mildly critical remarks about Ardern's handling of the crisis on Facebook. Playing politics was seriously out of fashion.

In her first campaign ad, Collins essentially advocated the same policy mix as Ardern – for example, infrastructure and "a greener, smarter future" – saying communities, livelihoods and futures were at stake. Her problem, of course, was that Ardern had built record levels of trust in her leadership through the pandemic.

And when voters went to the polls on 17 October, they delivered a result which must reverberate for politicians around the world. Not only did Ardern win handsomely, but she also became the first prime minister to win a majority in her own right under the MMP system: Labour would now have the opportunity to enact its agenda however it wanted. It was an echo of the previous realities of government power under the old system that her predecessor Geoffrey Palmer had described all those years ago as an elected dictatorship.

And it is noteworthy that it was that sense of decisive leadership from the top down that so appealed. Yes, Ardern is something of a rarity in politics. People think she's actually nice. And kind. But it is also the case that the history of her prime ministership created a number of rare opportunities to assert national leadership, rather than just political leadership. And voters responded. It blew away all the humdrum of political controversy and scandal, and failed policy delivery, that were the stuff of much of the daily reporting of her first term in government.

In 2017, she had promised change and spoken of "kindness" and "hope." The government in 2019 had introduced a first "Wellbeing Budget," which focused on mental-health issues, child wellbeing, supporting Māori and Pasifika community aspirations, as well as addressing New Zealand's stubbornly low productivity rates and pushing for more sustainable economic outcomes.

Whatever the failures to achieve those things in her first term, when it came to her response to the attacks on two Christchurch mosques in March 2019, and then in response to COVID, there was a reassuring continuity of language and approach. By acting decisively and early, when the global crisis – particularly as it was hitting Europe – was at its most frightening, she was able to enlist widespread political support. It became a national response, not a political one. The absence of state governments didn't just mean she was spared the job of negotiating and coordinating with another level of government; she was also spared a second tier of political leaders who might have had more local, or different, messages.

All the comparisons with what happened in Australia seem fairly conspicuous. Scott Morrison did not have the advantage of being a clearly defined type of leader to voters at the time of the pandemic, except perhaps through his disastrous handling of the bushfire catastrophe that swept through eastern Australia over the summer of 2019–20. While much of his response to the coronavirus made amends for that, by being based on the advice of experts and moving quickly, there remained the prevarication and attempts at trade-offs which clouded the message. His early national and collaborative leadership with the states and territories deteriorated as time passed, and as he and his ministers embarked on a "start–stop" move into political mode in their responses to the states, particularly Queensland and Victoria.

And it seemed that even in the middle of a crisis, the Coalition could not resist seizing opportunities to prosecute culture wars against institutions such as the university sector, despite international education being our fourth-largest export. Convoluted explanations were given for leaving some of the areas hardest hit by the pandemic – such as higher education, and arts and entertainment – without properly thought-through assistance. This undermined the government's case that it was running policy on a national, rather than political, basis.

But it required more than just popularity to carry the population when Ardern locked the country down in March 2020. For when they said lockdown in New Zealand, they really meant it. No going out even to get a takeaway coffee. It was radical, and it was fast, and it happened while other countries were still thinking about it.

The economic impact of the different approaches taken in Australia and New Zealand was clear: the New Zealand economy contracted 1.3 per cent in the March quarter, compared to just 0.3 per cent in Australia. And while GDP shrunk another 7 per cent in Australia in the June quarter, it plummeted 12 per cent in New Zealand. (This, of course, is before the Australian economic numbers became mired in the effects of the COVID outbreak in Victoria.)

An economy shrinking by 12 per cent is a pretty staggering figure to see, and it was the number still in Kiwi minds when they went to the polls on 17 October. The test of which approach had done the least damage would come in the shape and size of the economic recovery in the two countries as 2020 ended and there was more chance to survey the long-term damage in 2021.

With her election victory, her newfound authority and no obligation to negotiate with other parties, the real tests for Jacinda Ardern would begin. And while she had no need to form a coalition, the prime minister nonetheless held talks with the Greens about a consultation arrangement with the minor party, showing a sense of cooperation beyond the conceptual grasp of Australian politics.

Her careful approach to many policy issues in her first term was sometimes hard to read: was this due to the need for coalition compromise, or just caution? Now the difficult task awaited her of holding the country together while reopening an economy reliant on the movement of people. New Zealand's borders were still closed as the election drew near, in an economy in which tourism represented 20 per cent of the country's exports and around 6 per cent of GDP. Some 92,000 people had lost their jobs in the sector in 2020.

In Australia, federal and state governments have had an erratic record when it comes to transparency and keeping us informed of their thinking. By comparison, the Ardern government began a habit of voluntarily and pre-emptively releasing massive dumps of official cabinet papers and briefing notes through 2020, documenting the briefings it was receiving as COVID-19 first emerged, and the various options it considered in dealing with it.

Not only did New Zealand lock down harder, it also spent bigger to keep the economy afloat. By early September, the government had announced spending totalling NZ$62.1 billion – equivalent to 21.3 per cent of GDP – through to 2023–24. By comparison, federal measures in Australia amounted to A$180.9 billion – or 9.3 per cent of GDP through to 2023–24. In addition, state and territory governments announced stimulus packages amounting to A$369 billion, or 1.9 per cent of GDP, including payroll tax relief and discounts on utility bills. Both countries introduced wage subsidies worth just over 5 per cent of GDP.

Where the responses differed was in New Zealand's decision to make many of the changes permanent. And so the discussion did not immediately become focused on when the support would stop, which undermined confidence and certainty in Australia.

There was a permanent increase in social spending on protecting vulnerable people, including the disabled, worth 0.8 per cent of GDP, as well as income relief payments for people who had lost their jobs (amounting to 0.2 per cent of GDP). There were also permanent changes in business taxes to help cashflow, costing around 1 per cent of GDP.

There was support for aviation, tourism and government housing. There was an increase in base funding for the national public broadcaster, Radio New Zealand, "to support current levels of service, including essential journalism, news and media."

There was also early concern to assist the significant number of international students in the country, noting, apart from anything else, the potential damage to the reputation of the nation as an education provider. This is in marked contrast with Australia's appalling, and extraordinarily unremarked-upon, decision to abandon around one million temporary visa holders – including not just international students and refugees, but longer-term residents who had been invited to Australia to fill skills shortages on temporary visas – leaving them without any form of government assistance.

Notably, arts and culture were recognised as playing a crucial economic, as well as cultural, role in New Zealand and they have seen a continuous rollout of support since the pandemic struck. Ardern registered in May that the cultural sector "was amongst the worst hit by the global pandemic ... Now more than ever we need a thriving arts and cultural sector. We saw in the aftermath of the Canterbury earthquakes the potential of creativity and culture to create jobs, drive economic recovery and enhance social wellbeing, and they can help us do it again."

When the Morrison government finally decided to offer support to the arts sector during 2020, it went to almost bizarre lengths to try to hide the fact. Support for the "entertainment" industry was announced at that bastion of high arts, Rooty Hill in Sydney's west. It was defended as support for the "tradies" who worked backstage. And yet the irony was that the only money going out the door immediately was to organisations funded by the Australia Council – the very high arts organisations which would ostensibly be the targets of a government that liked to portray the arts as something for the elites, by the elites.

June 2020 saw much of New Zealand life return to some form of normality. Despite an outbreak of COVID in Auckland in August, which delayed the election campaign for a month, economists were predicting a strong rebound in the economy for the September quarter. It was this sense of confidence that Ardern was able to bring to the 2020 election campaign. In Australian reporting, and indeed international reporting generally, the success of the New Zealand coronavirus response has been inextricably bound up with the Ardern phenomenon: the young leader who leapt to global prominence in 2017, after taking the Labour leadership just seven weeks before the last New Zealand election.

Yet if Jacinda Ardern was an unknown to the rest of the world, she was not to New Zealanders. She'd long been positioned as a rising star in Labour ranks, a sign of youthful vitality in a party lost in the doldrums of almost a decade in opposition. She'd been given an exceptionally high spot on the party ticket (a bit like Senate tickets in Australia) that got her into parliament in 2008, and did not win an electorate in her own right until a February 2017 byelection, a few months before her elevation to the leadership. Ardern was well known to the public from her regular "Young Guns" spot on breakfast television, akin to the Joe Hockey–Kevin Rudd spot of old, against Simon Bridges, who would be one of the three opposition leaders who faced off against Ardern during her first term.

In sharp contrast with both Turnbull and Morrison, she came to the leader's job with clean hands: her predecessor, Andrew Little, stood down following disastrous polling figures; Ardern had only ever been in Opposition, so had no ministerial legacy to frame voters' views. She brought to the leadership a promise of "relentless positivity," but the same policies that Little had long been pledging: a solution to New Zealand's housing crisis, ending child poverty, more spending on health, cutting back immigration, which was "outpacing infrastructure," and cleaning up the country's polluted rivers. Perhaps ironically, even at the end of 2019 the media questioned whether Ardern would be able to win again, given her government's failure to deliver on many of these policies.

FULL CIRCLE

We started this story of Australia and New Zealand with Britain's Brexit decision and how it showed that once-great country coming full circle from a decision it took in the late 1960s to join the European Common Market, and thus to cast our two countries adrift.

As Jacinda Ardern was enjoying her smashing electoral victory in October 2020, the hapless figure of Boris Johnson was mired in an incompetent COVID response and, twelve months from that day in Umbria, his ongoing failure to chart a path out of Europe.

But there is another story of a full circle in this essay which comes out as we reflect on the arcs we have followed through New Zealand history, and the parallel story of what was happening in Australia.

Ardern was celebrating her fourth birthday on 26 July 1984, when David Lange and his government were sworn into office. Her early childhood had been spent in one of those towns so decimated by Rogernomics. Murupara was a small, isolated town which once boasted a large population of forestry and millworkers, but subsequently became infamous for gang violence and high levels of economic deprivation.

Thrown into the leadership weeks before the 2017 election, Ardern was leading a party promising to remedy some of the damage done. Labour actually won fewer seats, and a lesser share of the vote, than National at that election, but was able to secure the support of New Zealand First's Winston Peters to form a government. The comments of the contrarian, protectionist and long-serving MP when he finally came to reveal which major party he would back reflected that sense of accounts needing to be balanced after decades of change. "Far too many New Zealanders have come to view today's capitalism not as their friend but as their foe, and they are not all wrong," Peters said. "Capitalism must resume a human face."

*

Critics, particularly in Australia, have blamed the adoption in New Zealand of mixed-member proportional voting for the end of significant reform. That tends to jumble up cause and effect. It ignores the scars from the economic upheaval which helped create the conditions for MMP in the first place, and their underlying role in pushing both parties into the centre, and towards messages of continuity rather than change.

There have now been several shifts of power between coalitions led by Labour and National since MMP began in 1996, and there has been a reluctance to dramatically undo, or reshape, the central positions advanced by either side, whether they be on economic, foreign or even climate policy.

MMP forces political parties to negotiate clear positions before they form a government in cases where large coalitions have to be constructed. The process means all players enter government knowing what the agreements are; and, equally, that major parties' positions are tested. The hard negotiations take place when governments are formed, not later in a shifting series of Senate allegiances, as in Australia.

And change has still occurred. For the free-market advocates, that has included a new round of tax reforms under John Key – cutting income tax and lifting the GST – relying on the support of minor parties. Helen Clark, who had to manage a much more unwieldy coalition than Key, was also able to get significant social policy changes through the parliament.

The crucial factors – not unsurprisingly – are just how unwieldy any coalition might be and how effective the prime minister of the day is in leading a debate. In other words, the same factors that determine Australian governments' capacity to bring about change.

Clark points to one of the transformative changes brought about by MMP which has a resonance for our own politics. This is that the system forces the major parties into the middle. You cannot win unless you command the middle. Yet the more extreme ends of the spectrum are more conspicuously accommodated and represented by the minor parties. However, the major parties don't have to compete for votes with the more extreme elements at either end of the spectrum, as happens in Australia, where the major parties rely on minor-party preferences.

For example, National has not had to compete for votes with the ultra-free-market party ACT New Zealand, which came back from oblivion to claim a swag of seats in 2020.

Sure, MMP may mean you have to form a coalition, and a sometimes unwieldy one, with minor parties. But those minor parties are more akin to natural allies than competitors for votes. In the meantime, your policies are not being dragged out of the centre, as they are in Australia as a result of preferential voting.

MMP, Clark says, has ensured New Zealand politics has been civilised. And it has made for continuity. The major parties seldom undo each other's significant reforms, other than perhaps when it comes to industrial relations. The only risk in this analysis, she concedes, lies in weaknesses in the party system which let more radical elements in, and potentially allow them to take over more central positions.

MMP not only transformed how politics operated in New Zealand, but what both cabinet and parliament looked like. Māori representation and women's representation have at least doubled since 1996. But its deepest impact – compared to the way Australian politics has developed – has been in keeping the politics pragmatically civilised: you never know when you might have to talk to the party across the aisle.

There are always other players in any national discussion, of course. We have seen, for example, what a crucial role the Business Roundtable played in New Zealand at various times. The public service, despite all the privatisation that has gone on, is regarded with some envy by its Australian counterparts: senior public servants in Australia who deal regularly with their Kiwi counterparts say the service there has maintained its sense of independence, and is respected as a major contributor to advice, much more than has been the case in Australia. Ministerial offices in New Zealand have grown, but they have not supplanted the official channels of advice, as so often now happens here.

There is also a different attitude to transparency that goes way beyond Ardern's extraordinary (by Australian standards) voluntary document drop on the coronavirus response. For a start, the prime minister of the day has a regular press conference after each Monday cabinet meeting and reports on what cabinet discussed! Not just the "announceables," but what is under consideration by the government.

Perhaps most conspicuously different in the New Zealand political conversation is the structure of the media. Rupert Murdoch was once in New Zealand as the owner *The Dominion* in Wellington, but got out. The interests and influence of his empire in New Zealand now mainly come from the presence of the broadcaster Sky News. But his organisation does not control the national media debate as it does here. Historically, that partly reflects the fact that New Zealand does not have a national newspaper. "We don't have an equivalent of *The Australian*," Clark notes, adding that whenever she goes through an Australian airport and picks up a copy, she can only shake her head and breathe a sigh of relief.

Not having a national newspaper means there has not been a dominant voice setting the agenda, a force for hegemony of views. New Zealand is still served by newspapers based in its various cities.

A near-apoplectic tone to some of the commentary in Australia about Ardern's victory makes a telling statement about our respective political debates. *The Australian* thundered that "Ms Ardern should be under no illusions about the challenges she faces. As economics editor Adam Creighton wrote on Saturday, New Zealand 'in the space of half a year has blown its savings, smashed its two pistons of economic growth – tourism and immigration – and embarked on one of the world's most ambitious money creation programs.'" That this is exactly what has happened in the Australian economy as a result of Australian government policy seemed to escape the newspaper, which admonished the New Zealand prime minister that she must "honour her pledge to 'govern from the centre.'"

The paper also carried an almost hysterical opinion piece from the head of the conservative think-tank the Institute of Public Affairs, which shrilly warned that "she's a brilliant politician, but has been a grossly incompetent administrator. And with her seismic re-election on Saturday, New Zealand is in for a dangerous three years." The piece went on to quote Oliver Hartwich, chief executive of the IPA's Kiwi equivalent – and successor to the Business Roundtable – the New Zealand Initiative: "There is a distinct chance that if we don't sort out our economic challenges quickly, New Zealand could end up a failed state."

In *The Australian Financial Review*, under the heading "Why Jacinda Ardern is just like a Latin American populist," the columnist opined that it was "a bitter irony that after three years without progress on the core of its policy agenda, but after a historic electoral victory and with a commanding parliamentary majority, Ardern's Labour Party now faces greater obstacles to generating economic growth and moderating wealth inequality than when first taking power in 2017." No mention was made of where those problems of economic growth and wealth inequality might have started.

Public broadcasting also plays a very different role in New Zealand than in Australia. If there is one area where even some of the architects of privatisation and corporatisation concede they stuffed up, it is in public broadcasting, and it is one of the few areas of policy that keeps getting disrupted by changes of government.

The simple version of the story is that the equivalent of ABC Television, TVNZ, has had mostly to provide its own funding, through advertising, since 1989, and has had an erratic history of responsibility for the concept of public broadcasting. The equivalent of ABC Radio, on the other hand, Radio New Zealand, has kept its focus squarely on public broadcasting, and on news, current affairs and documentaries. There have been various proposals over the years, including in 2020, to recreate a more comprehensive public broadcasting service out of TVNZ and RNZ.

Recently, New Zealand media has diversified, much more than in Australia, into really comprehensive web-based news sites, particularly given the size of the national market, including Stuff (variously owned by News Corp Australia, and then what was Fairfax, but bought out by its chief executive in 2020). There is also *Newsroom* and *The Spinoff*, as well as *The Guardian*. While representing unapologetic political positions, they generally do not engage in the culture wars that have become endemic in the Australian media.

And this brings us to one of the most interesting themes that I think lurks in so many aspects of this story: competition and monopoly. Australia and New Zealand have both been the poorer at times for a lack of competition over ideas in political circles or the media debate. The failures of radical free-market economics to improve our welfare or productivity have been due to usually unrecognised limits to its efficacy in small markets, where privatisation will lead to monopolies and anti-competitive behaviour or to problems of lack of scale. New Zealand is another relatively small economy with a relatively narrow economic base, and the problems of adjusting to a more exposed global position have been exacerbated by a relatively small number of options, investors and power bases.

For all the criticisms of MMP and its restraint on reform – either the conservative push for even more deregulation, or the Labour ambition for progressive policies – it has ultimately not hindered the power of a New Zealand prime minister.

The capacity of New Zealand's leaders to change their country in a variety of different institutional settings must inevitably raise questions about how big an impediment our own structures really are to change. We hear so often that the problem is the Senate, or the states. But do the experiences of New Zealand rather play to the argument that what has been lacking in Australia on many occasions has been both political skill and leadership?

The New Zealand story also points to the issues we have put in the too-hard basket that shouldn't be there, such as Indigenous recognition and reconciliation, and issues we scarcely seem to acknowledge. While inequality has been a lightning-rod issue in recent New Zealand elections, the reality is that inequality in Australia is on some measures greater than in New Zealand, or at least on par with it.

The global pandemic of 2020 has given Australia and New Zealand a new reason to appreciate their economic relationship. While both countries have prospered and grown on the back of the rise of China, they now confront a future where China is a more menacing strategic shadow and a less certain source of economic prosperity. For now, China as a source of international students and tourists is in question, to say nothing of its uncertain status as a booming market for our merchandise.

Instead, we have found our leaders looking to each other – and a trans-Tasman bubble – as we seek to re-emerge into a world defined for the present by the constrictions of COVID-19. New Zealand's cabinet documents, in discussing a survival strategy for the country's tourism industry, note that "Australia may be able to fill some of the gap left by other markets."

It is not just one-way traffic. New Zealanders represent a huge proportion of our annual tourism trade, a fact that tends to be overlooked amid waves of excitement about whichever new nation is filling our hotels and holiday destinations.

Talk of the need to shorten supply chains must inevitably raise the question of the extent to which our two countries should start to consider closer ties in other sectors. Similarly, the changing dynamics of COVID and the region give us all the more reason to collaboratively use our different skills and focus in a strategic sense: not just what to do about opening up as a pandemic rages, but what to do about China in the Pacific, tapping into New Zealand's different perspective on the region.

Size (both geographical and population), climate and resources mean there are fundamental differences in our economies. But we have both faced a unique tyranny of distance from the rest of the world since white settlement.

The mantras that dominate Australian politics now are just as entrenched as the ones which once endorsed centralised wage-fixing and high tariff barriers. They are so entrenched they are almost unspoken, but often couched in Australia in the mode of thwarted ambition rather than philosophical endpoints: government spending should be lower; taxes should be lower; government does things worse than the private sector; there are too many blocks to development; the wages system is not flexible enough.

If COVID-19 has taught us anything, it is the hollowness of many of these presumptions. But even before the pandemic there were big questions. Does deregulation of a market necessarily give good outcomes if the likely structure of the privatised or deregulated market is likely to be the replacement of a public-sector monopoly with a private-sector one? Do we know what those changes will lead to, above and beyond what we think they are trying to fix?

There was a long period of national self-flagellation in New Zealand – as in Australia – about the economy in the 1980s, marked by an obsession with cutting government spending and the withdrawal of government from the economy. The social cost of a more radical form of neoliberalism in New Zealand can be seen across the country, in its decimation of local communities, in the growing inequality which built into a major source of political pressure as the pandemic hit, producing the Ardern phenomenon. For all that pain, the best that can be said is that New Zealand has ended up with economic outcomes about the same as Australia's.

Strong economic growth in the past decade in New Zealand has helped build national confidence, as did the end of the Brain Drain, which saw so many people voting with their feet and leaving. This occurred alongside a rising national pride in finding an independent voice on foreign policy.

While Māori disadvantage remains as much an eyesore as Indigenous disadvantage in Australia, New Zealand has embraced its indigenous culture over the past thirty years – and become both comfortable with and proud of it – in a way we have not.

We have had an experiment, a point of comparison, in all these things occurring across the Tasman all these years, if we just chose to look.

GRAPHS

The gap between the income earned by individual Australians and New Zealanders has widened (Figure 1).

The economies of both Australia and New Zealand were exceptionally volatile in the period up to the Australian recession of the early 1990s. Since then, Australian growth has both stabilised and stayed relatively strong, while New Zealand growth has remained much more volatile and prone to sudden downturns, until the last ten years when population growth started to add to New Zealand's growth (Figure 2).

Figure 3 is a shorter-term graph than many of the others but demonstrates the much greater slice of the New Zealand labour market that is absorbed by tourism – and what a risk COVID-19 therefore poses to the smaller nation's economic outlook.

The removal of industry protection and subsidies and the more radical deregulation of the labour market have gradually eroded relative wages in New Zealand, sparking the so-called "Brain Drain" to Australia as workers have sought better returns in an easily accessible alternative market (Figure 4).

As Australia starts to comprehend the potential impact that the sudden drop in population growth that flows from migration will have on our economy, we can look to New Zealand to see how its struggle to hold on to its people has restrained economic growth (Figure 5).

Measures of inequality vary between Australia and New Zealand. But while inequality has become a huge political issue in New Zealand, the same cannot be said of Australia (Figure 6).

The Gini coefficient (Figure 7) is a number which seeks to represent how far a country's income distribution varies from a completely equitable one. The higher the Gini coefficient, the greater the degree of inequality.

Figure 1: *Annual GNI per capita (USD 000s), 1970–2019*

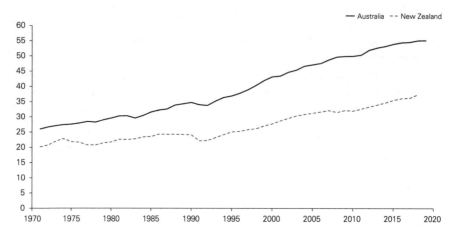

Note: expressed in US 2010 prices

Source: World Bank, AlphaBeta Analysis

Figure 2: *Annual GDP, percentage of year on year growth, 1971–2019*

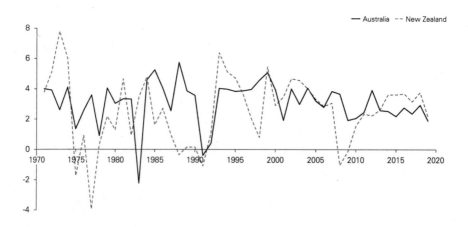

Source: World Bank, AlphaBeta Analysis

Figure 3: Percentage of total employed persons who are employed in tourism, 2003–20

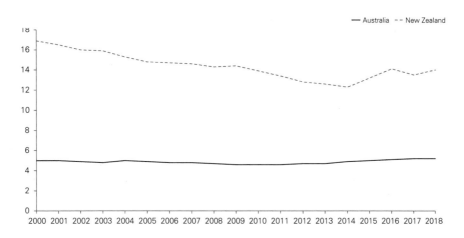

Source: ABS Cat. 5249, Statistics NZ, Alphabeta Analysis

Figure 4: Relative wages over time (wage price index), 1998–2020

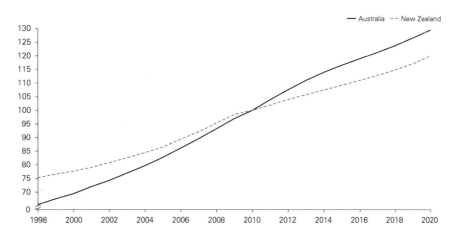

Note: includes private and public wages
Source: ABS Cat. 5249, Statistics NZ, Alphabeta Analysis

Figure 5: Net overseas migration (000s), 2006–19

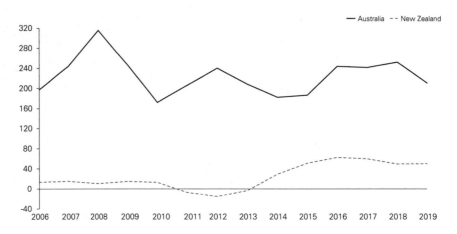

Note: Data has been taken from 2006 onwards to ensure like-for-like comparison between net overseas migration in Australia and New Zealand under the 12/16 rule
Source: ABS Cat. 3412, Statistics NZ, Alphabeta Analysis

Figure 6: Percentage share of total income earnt by the top 1 percentile, 1970–2019

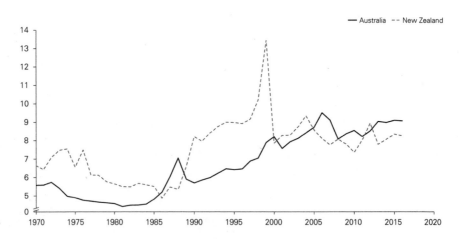

Source: World Inequality Database, Alphabeta Analysis

Figure 7: Gini coefficient, 1981–2014

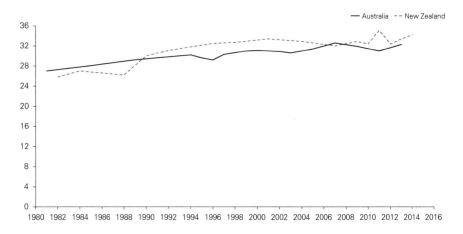

Note: Gaps in data have been interpreted

Source: World Inequality Database, Alphabeta Analysis

Figure 8: Budget balance as a percentage of GDP, 1990–2019

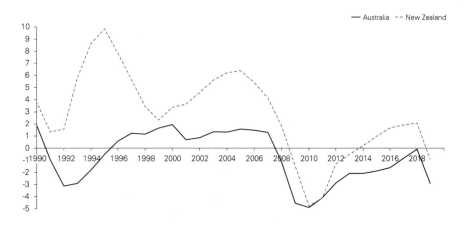

Source: IMF, Alphabeta Analysis

SOURCES

The writing of this essay didn't quite go to plan in 2020: further planned trips to New Zealand for face-to-face interviews were shelved as borders closed, and the subject matter itself had to shift to accommodate the pandemic, meaning some issues that I had really wanted to delve into had to be dropped. Even the essay itself went on hold for a brief period in the early days of the pandemic: who would be interested in New Zealand in such times, we thought!

Despite the travel restrictions, I got to talk to a lot of people in New Zealand before the gates closed, and a lot more afterwards via the technologies that have become ubiquitous.

I want to express my deep gratitude to the politicians, bureaucrats, national security experts, political staff, academics, economists and community advocates, past and present, on both sides of the Tasman, who shared their thoughts with me and pointed me in the direction of people, reading and research.

I would particularly like to acknowledge the wealth of understanding I gained, and which I think has enriched the essay, from James Belich's *Paradise Reforged: A history of the New Zealanders*; from Denis McLean's *The Prickly Pear: Making nationalism in Australia and New Zealand*; from Shireen Morris's "Lessons from New Zealand: Towards a better working relationship between indigenous peoples and the state"; and from Guyon Espiner and Tim Watkin's *The Ninth Floor: Conversations with five New Zealand prime ministers*.

Andrew Charlton at AlphaBeta Advisors was particularly generous in assigning the extraordinarily obliging, patient and diligent Kasun Yakupityage to research comparable historic economic data and put it into a massive series of graphs for me to use as a constant visual check of how Australia's and New Zealand's economies evolved. We included just a few of these at the end of the essay.

I am particularly grateful to Justin Stevens, my executive producer at 7.30, who not only gave me time off to write, but, as in all things, was a source of constant support and encouragement for the essay.

My family and friends will be eternally grateful that they no longer have to have perfectly innocent conversations broken up by fascinating facts about New Zealand. But I am eternally grateful that they were always able at least to act interested.

For the good friends who urged me, even piggybacked me, through what unexpectedly proved a very rough few last miles of the road, particularly Jenny Morris, Helen Trinca and my darling Tosca Ramsey.

And for Sam Neill.

Taku Toroa koroirangi ka tau ki te whenua ka kau ki Aotearoa, Tauaru ai au ki reira.

1 "If community transmission", "These decisions", "I am not": Claire Trevett, "Five big moments that changed politics", *The New Zealand Herald*, 14 June 2020.

4 "Look, you read": Guyon Espiner and Tim Watkin, *The Ninth Floor: Conversations with five New Zealand prime ministers*, Bridget Williams Books and Radio New Zealand, August 2017.

5 "the effect of frustrating": "Supreme Court: Lady Hale's statement on 'unlawful' Parliament suspension", BBC (online), 24 September 2020.

9 "This misrepresents", "in doing so": James Belich, *Paradise Reforged: A history of the New Zealanders*, Penguin, 2002.

16 "average subsidy": Vangelis Vitalis, "Agricultural subsidy reform and its implications for sustainable development: The New Zealand experience", *Environmental Sciences*, vol. 4, no. 1, 20 March 2007, pp. 21–40.

18–19 "did not tell me" and "they had gone": David Lange, *My Life*, Penguin, 2006.

19 "it got the ball rolling": *Revolution*, television documentary, 1996, NZonscreen, www.nzonscreen.com/title/revolution-the-grand-illusion-1996.

21–2 "any decision", "a recurrent assertion", etc.: Nicholas Aroney, "New Zealand, Australasia and Federation', *Canterbury Law Review*, vol. 16, 2010, pp. 31–46.

23 "the Australians fashioned": Denis McLean, *The Prickly Pear: Making nationalism in Australia and New Zealand*, Otago University Press, 2003.

23 "The Australian" and "Australians tended": Tpr C. Pocok, Canterbury Mounted Rifles, diary, 25 March 1915, quoted in Christopher Pugsley, *Gallipoli: The New Zealand story*, Hodder & Stoughton, Auckland, 1984.

24 "New Zealand National myth": 'The Letters of Randolph Norman Gray' in Jock Phillips, Nicholas Boyack and E.P. Malone (eds), *The Great Adventure: New Zealand soldiers describe the First World War*, Allen & Unwin, Wellington, 1988, quoted in McLean, *The Prickly Pear*.

24 "New Zealanders and Australians": McLean, *The Prickly Pear*.

24 "Our ties": Address to the Parliament of New Zealand by Australian Prime Minister Julia Gillard, 17 February 2011.

28 "something like a cult of forgetfulness": W.E.H. Stanner, 1968 Boyer lectures.

29 "The version written in Māori": Nicola R. Wheen and Janine Hayward (eds), *Treaty of Waitangi Settlements*, Bridget Williams Books, 2012, Chapter 1.

29–30 "Views that saw", "The discriminatory view": Shireen Morris, "Lessons from New Zealand: Towards a better working relationship between Indigenous peoples and the state", *Australian Indigenous Law Review*, vol. 18, no. 2, 2014–15, p. 72.

31 "began to sketch": Mason Durie, *Te Mana, Te Kāwanatanga: The politics of Māori self-determination*, Oxford University Press, Auckland, 1998.

32 "It was greatly resisted": Palmer, quoted in Espiner and Watkin, *The Ninth Floor*.

32 "In the early days", "Māori were going to continue", "We needed a museum": Bolger, quoted in Espiner and Watkin, *The Ninth Floor.*

34 "dangerous drift" etc.: Don Brash, Speech, Orewa Rotary Club, 27 January 2004.

35 "You know": Clark, quoted in Espiner and Watkin, *The Ninth Floor.*

35 Key … regarded: Interview with close Key associate.

35 assessments of his period in office: Martin Fisher, "The leading contender for John Key's primary legacy? Treaty settlements", *The Spinoff*, 18 January 2017.

35–6 "Economic losses": Te Rūnanga o Ngāi Tahu, "Economic security", Te Rūnanga o Ngāi Tahu website, https://ngaitahu.iwi.nz/ngai-tahu/the-settlement/settlement-offer/economic-security/, accessed 31 October 2020.

36 around NZ$2.2 billion: NZ Ministry for Culuture and Heritage, "What are Treaty settlements and why are they needed?" Te Tai Treaty Settlement Stories, https://teara.govt.nz/en/te-tai/about-treaty-settlements, 31 October 2020.

36 NZ$7.8 billion: "Why New Zealand's Maori do better than Australia's Aboriginals", *The Economist*, 1 December 2018.

36 "divided public opinion": Wheen and Hayward, *Treaty of Waitangi Settlements.*

38 "was a game-changer": Megan Davis, "Reconciliation and the promise of an Australian homecoming", *The Monthly*, July 2020.

39 "established important": M. Gray and B. Hunter, "The comparative wellbeing of the New Zealand Māori and Indigenous Australian populations since 2000", *Lessons from New Zealand*, no. 116, 2017, p. 74.

42 "Shared history": New Zealand Department of Foreign Affairs and Trade, "Our relationship with Australia', MFAT, www.mfat.govt.nz/en/countries-and-regions/australia/, accessed 30 October 2020.

42 "Australia and New Zealand": Australian Department of Foreign Affairs and Trade, "New Zealand country brief", DFAT, www.dfat.gov.au/geo/new-zealand/Pages/new-zealand-country-brief, accessed 30 October 2020.

43 "There are other countries": Tony Abbott, Interview with Fran Kelly, *Breakfast*, Radio National, 11 February 2010.

44 "How can": Hockey, quoted in "Strewth mate, hold on a bit", *Stuff*, 17 May 2013.

44 "reflect a consistent pattern": John Quiggin, "The land of the long white mirage", *Inside Story*, 21 August 2013.

46 "his economic program": "2. The Grand Illusion", *Revolution,*

47 "We knew": Clark, quoted in Espiner and Watkin, *The Ninth Floor.*

47 "was not invited": "2. The Grand Illusion", *Revolution.*

48 "allowed them", "interest groups": Shaun Goldfinch, *Remaking Australian and New Zealand Economic Policy: Ideas, institutions and policy communities*, Georgetown University Press, 2001.

48   "They didn't actually": Lange, quoted in Goldfinch, p. 107.

50   Fay Richwhite & Company: Brian Gaynor, *New Zealand Herald*.

51   tax concessions and free government: Vitalis, "Agricultural subsidy reform" cites IMF, *New Zealand: Selected issues, country report*, No. 4/127, Washington: IMF, 2004; R.W.M. Johnston, *Reforming EU farm policy: Lessons from New Zealand*, Occasional Paper 112, London, Institute of Economic Affairs, 2000; NZ Ministry of Agriculture, *The New Zealand Reforms*, Paris, OECD 1996; NZ Ministry of Economic Development, *Growing an Innovative New Zealand*, Wellington: Ministry of Economic Development, 2001; NZ Treasury. *New Zealand's Economic Growth: An analysis of performance and policy*. Wellington, 2004; Statistics New Zealand, *The New Zealand Official Yearbook*. Wellington, 1984; Statistics New Zealand, *The New Zealand Official Yearbook 2001*, Wellington, 2002; Statistics New Zealand, *Agricultural Subsidy Reform in New Zealand*, 39, 2002; Statistics New Zealand. *Monitoring Progress Towards a Sustainable New Zealand*, Wellington, David Bateman Publications, 2002.

51   subsidies dropped: ibid. The OECD's Producer Subsidy Equivalent (PSE), which (as the name suggests) estimates the value of various subsidies to farmers, fell from an average of 24 per cent in 1979 to 3 per cent in 1989.

51   sheep flock: ibid. Less than a decade later in 1995, however, farmland values had recovered to around 86 per cent of their 1982 value, in real terms, and by 2007 had risen above 100 per cent of the 1982 figure.

52   the government had announced: The fire sale would eventually reap around NZ$16 billion: equivalent to just over two-thirds of government debt when Lange and Douglas came to office. Murray Dobbin, "New Zealand's vaunted privatization push devastated the country, rather than saving it", *The National Post* (Canada), 15 August 2000.

52   west coast figures: Greg Halseth, *Transformation of Resource Towns and Peripheries: Political economy perspectives*, Routledge, 2017.

52–3 estimated to be 76,000: Judith Bell, *I See Red: The shocking story of a battle against the warehouse*, AWA Press, June 2006.

53   fell by 30 per cent: Steven Stillman, Malathi Velamuri and Andrew Aitken, *The Long-Run Impact of New Zealand's Structural Reform on Local Communities*, Motu Working Paper 08-11, Motu Economic and Public Policy Research, July 2008.

54   inflation reduced: Even before the new inflation targeting policy was officially implemented, the inflation rate in 1987 had been 15.74 per cent in 1987 and fell to 6.38 per cent in 1988 as real interest rates were lifted and the New Zealand dollar rose sharply in value.

55   "As it got worse": Moore quoted in Espiner and Watkin, *The Ninth Floor*.

56   "several had been wiped out": "New Zealand companies need a period of calm", *Australian Financial Review*, 7 September 1990.

57   "Seventeen hours": Bolger quoted in Espiner and Watkin, *The Ninth Floor*.

57   "one-third of its loan": *Australian Financial Review*, 8 February 1990.

58   "fiscal deficit": Jane Kelsey, "New Zealand 'experiment' a colossal failure", *Converge*, 9 July 1999.

58   "harsh" or "oppressive": Jack Vowles, Hilde Coffe and Jennifer Curtin, *A Bark but No Bite: Inequality and the 2014 New Zealand election*, ANU Press, 2017.

59   "work longer hours" and "New Zealand's labour productivity": New Zealand Productivity Commission, "Productivity", New Zealand Government, www.productivity.govt.nz/productivity/, accessed 31 October 2020.

60   "it was going to reduce", "thought that", "Of course" and "MMP arrived": Palmer quoted in Espiner and Watkin, *The Ninth Floor*.

63   "ghastly period", "a huge preoccupation" and "People [had] voted": Clark quoted in Espiner and Watkin, *The Ninth Floor*.

64   "They were very, very aggressive": Clark quoted in Espiner and Watkin, *The Ninth Floor*.

64   "lost the plot": *Australian Financial Review*, quoted in Branko Marcetic, "Does Jacinda Ardern face a Helen Clark-style winter of discontent?", *The Spinoff*, 7 June 2018.

65–6 "The *Rainbow Warrior*" and "it is the price": Lange quoted in "Nuclear-free New Zealand", New Zealand History website, https://nzhistory.govt.nz/politics/nuclear-free-new-zealand/nuclear-free-zone, accessed 2 November 2020.

66   "to maintain a sense of usefulness": Author interview with official, February 2020.

67   "we would escort", "Immigration was very worried", "when the decision was made": Clark quoted in Espiner and Watkin, *The Ninth Floor*.

68   "Although both countries": Mark Thomson, "The Australia–New Zealand defence partnership: a net assessment", *The Strategist*, ASPI, 21 February 2018.

69–70 largely free: New Zealand has spent less than 1.4 per cent of its budget on defence since 2008. It spent just 1.1 per cent of GDP in 2018, compared to 1.9 per cent by Australia. It has budgeted NZ$110 million on intelligence and security in its 2020 budget. Mark Thomson, *New Zealand, Australia and the ANZUS Alliance: Interests, identity and strategy*, ASPI special report, February 2018.

69   Fonterra data: Global Rural, "Deconstructing the New Zealand dairy boom", www.global-rural.org/story_map/deconstructing-the-new-zealand-dairy-boom/, accessed 31 October 2020.

71   80 per cent renewable energy from hydroelectricity: Hamish Rutherford, "Experts warn 100pc renewable electricity target will hurt New Zealand's wider climate goals", Stuff, 24 January 2019.

72   35 per cent behind: John Quiggin, "How New Zealand fell further behind", *Inside Story*, 11 November 2015.

73   "Labour's complacency": Michael Jones in Paul t' Hart and Karen Tindall (eds), *Framing the Global Economic Downturn: Crisis rhetoric and the politics of recessions*, ANU Press, 2009, Chapter 10.

73   "it is not": "Recommendations: Response to global financial crisis", Business New Zealand, www.businessnz.org.nz/__data/assets/pdf_file/0010/74719/BusinessNZ-response-to-global-financial-crisis.pdf, accessed 31 October 2020.

75   "Australian bully boy": Jackson, quoted in Ben Child, "Peter Jackson threatens to take The Hobbit to eastern Europe", *Guardian Australia*, 27 September 2010.

75   "coming down to New Zealand": Jackson and Walsh, quoted in Tom Cardy and Kirsty Johnson, "Hobbit looks to be headed overseas", *Stuff*, 21 October 2020.

76   "Key announced": NBR, "Key comes through: $34m deal sees Hobbit stay in NZ", NBR.co.nz, 28 October 2010.

76   "behind the agreement": Michael Cieply and Jeremy Rose, "New Zealand bends and Hobbit stays", *The New York Times*, 28 October 2010.

76   "at some point": "Editorial: Price to keep Hobbit in New Zealand is extortionate", *New Zealand Herald*, 29 October 2010.

79   a number of firsts: Patrick Köllner, "Australia and New Zealand recalibrate their China policies: Convergence and divergence", *The Pacific Review*, 7 November 2019.

80   "took a fairly benign view": Köllner, "Australia and New Zealand recalibrate".

82   "decided to be at the table": Köllner, "Australia and New Zealand recalibrate".

83   "Extricating New Zealand": Anne-Marie Brady, "China 2.0 and the challenge it poses to New Zealand", *Noted*, 7 November 2018.

83   Yang Jian: Köllner, "Australia and New Zealand recalibrate".

83   "some of the biggest donors", etc.: Jamil Anderlini, "China is taking its ideological fight abroad", *Financial Times*, 9 January 2020.

84   "the New Zealand government": Anne-Marie Brady, "New Zealand's quiet China shift", *The Diplomat*, 1 July 2020.

91   "to support current levels": Grant Robertson, *Summary of Initiatives: In the COVID-19 Response and Recovery Fund (CRRF) foundational package*, Budget 2020, New Zealand Government.

91   "was amongst the worst-hit": "Government invests in New Zealand's cultural recovery", Media release by Jacinda Ardern and other ministers, 28 May 2020.

93   "Far too many New Zealanders": Peters, quoted in Michael Daly, "Winston Peters wants 'today's capitalism' to regain its 'human face'", *Stuff*, 20 October 2017.

96 "Ms Ardern": "Covid shaped New Zealand's election result", Editorial, *The Australian*, 18 October 2020.

97 "she's a brilliant politician": Gideon Rozner, "Danger across the ditch as incompetent leader Ardern wins", *The Australian*, 18 October 2020.

97 "a bitter irony": Henry Thomson, "Why Jacinda Ardern is just like a Latin American populist", *Australian Financial Review*, 20 October 2020.

David Marr

Pollsters and journalists weren't the only ones caught unawares last May. So were publishers. Nothing on Morrison hit the market before or after his miracle victory. No biographies charting his rise and, it must be said, no Quarterly Essay exploring his character. We didn't bother. It wasn't just that Morrison seemed destined to lose. There was something else, something we mistakenly thought would underwrite his loss: he wasn't interesting.

We knew enough about Morrison the man not to want to know more – the sackings, the happy clapper faith, the ugly scramble through the ranks to snatch preselection, his ambiguous role in the slaughter of Turnbull. But there wasn't much curiosity to know more. So despite the return of the Coalition government there was nothing in the shops from Allen & Unwin or Scribe or Black Inc. The verdict of the publishing trade was: adios.

His win was interesting. We've been picking over the victory ever since to see what it tells us about this country and its politics. But few would venture to find reasons for the Coalition's success in the character of Scott Morrison or his avatar ScoMo. This was a victory owed to technique not character. His win was fascinating but Morrison has remained stubbornly dull until now.

To Katharine Murphy are due the thanks of a grateful nation for producing a fascinating study of such an unrewarding subject. I've not read anything about Morrison so attentive, respectful and revealing. That she is left in the end quoting Gertrude Stein – "There is no there there" – is not an admission of defeat but a conclusion loaded with meaning.

She doesn't slam it down on the table. The Murphy technique is to take us with her as she thinks things through. We judge as we follow. She builds trust. She has a way – it's her tone – of reminding us that beyond the Canberra wrangling is a plain question that always matters: is all this decent?

Her portrait of Morrison is of a not-indecent machine man learning on the job to be prime minister. That takes time. It's assumed that prime ministers know what they're doing from day one. The truth is, the only place to learn that job is on the job. Kevin Rudd once told me it takes a term. He didn't get it. Nor did Gillard or Abbott or Turnbull. This one will at least have time.

He can learn. I remember the horrible press conferences he held as Minister for Immigration to beat up on the invasion of Australia by criminal hordes of asylum seekers. Beside him as a most uncomfortable piece of set decoration was General Angus Campbell. Neither man answered a single question that mattered.

What remains with me most vividly from that time was Morrison's smile as he refused to play ball. A smile is a valuable thing in politics; a good, easy smile is a vote-winner. But as he wouldn't say how many boats had been caught or how many refugees had drowned on the way, Morrison's smile was a little smile of victory: I'm not telling and you can't make me. It said: fuck off.

He can't do that in the pandemic and Murphy's account of how he has come to understand the need to be more inclusive, more informative is a fascinating case study of a man growing in the job. He is likely to be with us for some time, the first prime minister since John Howard to serve a few terms.

So we need to understand this man more, perhaps, than we have any of his recent predecessors. We will come back and back to Murphy's superb account of a politician with no back story, an advertising guy who doesn't believe in persuasion, a scrapper who can vanish at a moment's notice, and a deep blue conservative with no ideology.

There and not there.

After reporting a few prime ministers over the years, I'd add that Morrison is the best of them at not answering questions. That great professional John Howard was, of course, a superb non-answerer. But even he didn't bring to the job the panache that Morrison displays when in top form.

The problem we face living with this oddly durable leader is that we have already lost so much of our capacity to compel answers from our politicians. The news cycle rolls on, leaving lies and rubble in its wake. In a highly partisan political world, too few of us are willing to call out dishonesty, incompetence and sheer indecency wherever it lies. It's why, more than ever, we need Katharine Murphy and Quarterly Essays.

David Marr

Phillip Coorey

To those of us fortunate enough to have had a ringside seat to the unfolding of some of the most dramatic events in contemporary political history, Katharine Murphy's essay *The End of Certainty* should come with a warning. Kath's documentation of those initial days and weeks of chaos, during which the government struggled to find the bottom of the crisis while the rest of us hung on for the ride, is not only an important and compelling piece of work, it is also mildly trauma-inducing. At least to this writer.

There were days that seemed surreal. Still do. Such as 19 March, on which, as Murphy recollects, the government dropped its longstanding aversion to increasing the unemployment benefit and doubled it, just like that. Qantas was grounded and laid off thousands of employees, the dollar fell to near or below US$0.50, the Reserve Bank of Australia cut what was left of interest rates and trundled out more than $100 billion in cheap credit just to keep the banks lending – all by mid afternoon. Later that day, the government announced almost $1 billion to bolster staffing levels at aged-care facilities in anticipation of the virus taking hold among the elderly.

In my front-page story for *The Australian Financial Review*, which attempted to hoover up all that had occurred and contextualise it, that near-$1 billion was the last paragraph of a 1000-word news report. Such was the magnitude of events that day. And there were many others just as insane.

Only weeks before, the government had been nickel-and-diming every single spending decision, even those worth a few hundred thousand dollars, as part of its pre-coronavirus intention to return the budget to surplus. That surplus, of course, never eventuated. Scott Morrison, Josh Frydenberg and the government, along with the states, did what needed to be done to avert a national health crisis and to soften the blow of crippling economic shutdowns.

It was as though Morrison was made for the moment – and it is this that Kath so expertly captures. In his relatively short time in federal politics, Morrison has been the true fixer. In an audacious interview with Sky News some years ago, Christopher Pyne ascribed that title to himself as he tried to extricate himself from a policy mess of his own creation. We all laughed.

Morrison entered the parliament in 2007, when Kevin Rudd beat John Howard, and he became a minister in 2013, when Tony Abbott took back power from Labor. As a minister, Morrison cultivated a reputation as someone who was not particularly idealistic, but rather the sort of fellow you point at a problem, turn the key in his back and tell him to go fix it. In this vein, he "stopped the boats" and then, as social security minister, fixed up the pension policy mess that Abbott had bequeathed through the disastrous 2014 federal budget and its planned cuts. As treasurer, Morrison established the discipline to return the budget to surplus. His predecessors had each kept pushing back the target date for surplus, so he drew a line and decreed it would be 2019–20. He didn't quite get there, but a balance was achieved.

When Malcolm Turnbull fell, Morrison came up the middle and took the top job. Even though he did so by outplaying those on both sides of the coup, he still brought a sense of the fixer to the problem. The Liberal Party had been tearing itself apart for a decade due to the feud between Turnbull and Abbott, which Morrison derided as the "Muppet Show."

"Many years ago, I can recall," Morrison said, "I was listening to a presentation from General Norman Schwarzkopf, and he said this: 'When placed in command, take charge.'" And so he did. And furthermore, he did not discourage the departure of the foot soldiers of that era, among them Pyne and Julie Bishop. It was an exercise in cleansing the party of the internal rancour which had held it back for so long. He also showed he was not to be underrated, by friend or foe. As a colleague once perfectly observed, Morrison would follow you into a revolving door and exit ahead of you and you'd have no idea how it happened.

Before the coronavirus pandemic, Morrison and his government were facing criticism for lacking an agenda – with some justification, given it was, after all, a third-term government. Other than being determined to steer the economy back to surplus, it was hardly bristling with ideas. This was exacerbated by Morrison not being particularly visionary. No one has ever accused him of being a policy wonk.

When the pandemic struck, all that criticism went out the window. It was a situation that needed a fixer, and a bloody good one. Of course, not everything went to plan. If the government had its time again, it would do some things differently, such as unveil a wage subsidy before doubling the dole, thus preventing those catastrophic and morale-destroying queues outside Centrelink. But by and large, and certainly in terms relative to the rest of the world, we have been pretty well served over the past six months. Moreover, it was a crisis that needed a pragmatist, not an ideologue. This is where *The End of Certainty* is a must-read for anyone who thinks they have a handle on our prime minister.

We have all observed and written about how Morrison is a pragmatist much in the mould of John Howard – which, from the perspective of his opponents, makes him difficult to corral. I clearly remember an exasperated Opposition leader Kim Beazley, after being outfoxed by Howard on something or other, exclaiming that trying to best Howard was akin to "trying to catch a fruit bat by the tail." Morrison is, as Kath details, ruthlessly transactional and just as pragmatic as Howard, but even less of an ideologue. Howard could backflip as well as the next guy but he had his shibboleths, namely tax reform and industrial relations.

"I'm a problem-solver," Morrison told Kath, before amending a principle often espoused by Peter Costello: "They say good policy is good politics. Well, actually, good problem-solving is even better. That is what I mean by suspending ideology – you've got to find the right answer." When Morrison and ministers were shovelling hundreds of billions out the door in assistance, stimulus and loans, Morrison cautioned us not to confuse such actions with an ideological shift. "Why did I do JobKeeper and JobSeeker? Because the security of the country was under threat. I wasn't setting up for some long-term welfare program." But he showed he will do whatever is necessary, as required.

Between the writing of Kath's essay and the writing of this response, Morrison handed down a recovery budget festooned with Labor policies. It was an updated and refined version of Paul Keating's 1992 One Nation blueprint designed to bust the recession. The key flaw with Keating's offering was that it was too late. Aside from that, Morrison and Frydenberg pretty much aped it – tax cuts to boost aggregate demand, wage subsidies to encourage hiring the unemployed, skills and training incentives, and, still to come, industrial relations flexibility (but nothing even approaching WorkChoices).

If he had wanted to embrace ideology, Morrison could have opted for company-tax cuts instead of the $27 billion investment allowance, which enables businesses to write off the full value of an asset in a bid to get them spending. This was a policy similar to that Labor took to the last election. Similarly, the budget brought forward the stage-two tax cuts Labor supports, but not the more generous and expensive stage-three cuts Labor does not support. Morrison took the path of least resistance in the budget. His aim was to fix the problem, not create intractable Senate battles over tax policy. Morrison even brought the ACTU into the tent to help with both crisis management and IR policy reform. It is understood Howard thought this a bridge too far. Morrison is – at the other end of the spectrum – the antithesis of Abbott, who always believed a fight was better than a fix.

As we emerge from the crisis and walk the long road to fixing the economic mess, Kath poses the fundamental question, which is the crux of her piece: "The economic recovery required after COVID will define a Morrison project, events will demand that. But going in, it is difficult to identify Morrison's abiding objectives in public life. What hill would Scott Morrison die on? Howard died on the hill of WorkChoices, losing his seat at the 2007 election."

It is a brilliantly clarifying question, and it must be one that Anthony Albanese and Labor are pondering. They thought they had Morrison pinned after his ham-fisted handling of the bushfires. But Morrison used the coronavirus to show he had learned. He did what he didn't do during the fires: listened to the experts and acted decisively and pre-emptively.

In as little as a year, he will be seeking for the Coalition a fourth term in office. But Morrison gives the impression of just getting started.

Phillip Coorey

Elizabeth Flux

I can see why something that was originally intended to be a profile of Scott Morrison evolved into a larger meditation on the politics of the pandemic – there is not enough of Morrison that can be pinned down on paper.

Seeing how a crisis of this scale affects politics – and individual politicians – has been fascinating, and Katharine Murphy's essay is a vivid dissection of the people at the core of our country's response. What it revealed, or rather didn't reveal, about the man at the top made me feel uncomfortable and worried.

In a crisis, things are thrown into sharp relief. All that is unnecessary is (or at least should be) stripped away as we focus on what matters. As individuals living in Australia, we have evaluated what we can sacrifice for the good of the country. Social lives. Hobbies. Seeing family. Many businesses have been forced to let go of the notion that physical presence is a vital element of commitment to a job. Maybe working from home isn't a last resort. Perhaps that meeting could actually be an email. And in politics, as Murphy's essay explores, are we finally seeing petty issues and partisanship put aside for the greater good?

In some cases, sure. The unusual partnerships brought out by the earliest stages of the pandemic did, fleetingly, provide a glimpse of this. But the deeper problem is that, for many, the business of politics is simply to *stay* in politics. The picture painted, from the few brushstrokes our PM would allow, is of a transactional man – a description of his own choosing – who is motivated by his own career.

For me, in an ideal world politics would be a-partisan. But I realise this is fundamentally impossible. And so, in the real world, the separation of parties should be by ideology, with individuals willing to let go of their own needs for the bigger goals they are working towards.

This does not describe Scott Morrison. The essay asks what hill Morrison would die on, and, reading between the lines, the answer seems clear: his own.

The theme of who is useful to Morrison comes up again and again. Not useful to the country. Not even to the party. To the individual. "I wasn't useful to him, so I wasn't a person he cultivated," Murphy writes.

Murphy's assessment of how Morrison's failures in the bushfires shaped his pandemic response was particularly interesting. Is he doing better now because he wants to do the right thing and be a stronger leader, or is it because he simply wants to be re-elected? The fact that this is a question at all is concerning. No matter how much someone says they are putting aside politics for the greater good, if we don't know what their definition of the greater good is, what it is they are working for, that is a problem.

I don't want an ideologue who can't shift their views or actions for the greater good, but I think it is equally or even more dangerous to have someone so motivated by the trajectory of their own career. Can you truly act in the civic interest and make hard decisions if you have an eye on the polls at all times? No.

We've seen this in Morrison refusing to talk about climate change in the context of the Black Summer bushfires. We've seen it in the groups excluded from financial support during the pandemic. And we've seen it in cutting back Job-Keeper when it is still needed, because a conservative government will always want to appeal to its conservative voters − in order to stay in power. Bigger, harder decisions will never be made, and necessary conversations will continue to be put off when politicians are driven by re-election.

The essay says Morrison is a populist. Watching him from Melbourne, I notice he is quick to swoop in and bask in reflected success, and he is equally fast to condemn when it might curry favour. He swiftly raked Australia Post over the coals for behaviour that, if engaged in by someone useful to him, might have seen him ringing the police commissioner for support. What is his underlying ideology or ethical drive beyond what is good for him as an individual?

Motivation matters. And with Morrison it feels that when push comes to shove, he will swing whichever way will best serve his political longevity or ultimate career goals. In a crisis this is terrifying.

Government can't be apolitical but we do need to know what we are getting, particularly from someone in the top job. When we have a prime minister who is primarily motivated by their own political survival, that will inevitably compromise their approach, make them fickle in the worst of ways.

As well as offering a glimpse of what could be, Australia's handling of the pandemic, despite the many successes, has actually revealed a deeper problem: with Morrison, there has never been any certainty − just the prioritising of image over action and long-term consequence.

Elizabeth Flux

Dominic Kelly

In calling her Quarterly Essay *The End of Certainty*, Katharine Murphy gives a knowing nod to Paul Kelly's identically titled classic of Australian political journalism, first published in 1992. It's an odd choice. Kelly was referring to the era-defining destruction of the "Australian Settlement" that had determined Australian policy settings since Federation: White Australia, industry protection, wage arbitration, state paternalism and imperial benevolence. By contrast, I don't think anyone could argue that the upheaval brought on by the coronavirus pandemic, devastating though it has been, brings to an end any kind of certainty. The story of the past decade of Australian politics has been one of near-constant crisis and *uncertainty*, illustrated most obviously by our extraordinary prime ministerial churn, but also evident in the precariousness of many Australians' lives long before the onset of COVID-19.

So the title felt like a misnomer, but as I read the essay I kept being reminded of Kelly, in the sense of Judith Brett's memorable description in Quarterly Essay 78: "Australia's very own Vicar of Bray ... never far from the orthodoxies of the powerful." Because although Murphy strains to demonstrate her bona fides as a watchful political analyst, what struck me most about the essay was its willingness to uncritically absorb Scott Morrison's spin about his pragmatic, non-ideological approach to the present crisis. This stems, we are told, from his experience as a party director more interested in solving problems than – in the vein of his mentor John Howard – changing the country to align with his political philosophy:

> Morrison doesn't rhapsodise about "reform." At his core, he's a populist, and a fixer, not an ideologue. He finds shibboleths, the core philosophical mantras of some of his centre-right predecessors and contemporary colleagues, boring, tired, tedious, claustrophobic.

Party directors are project managers, and it is helpful to think of Morrison as a project manager rather than the keeper of an ideological flame.

Coincidentally, Paul Kelly repeatedly asserted a similar view of Morrison and his government in *The Australian* before and after October's delayed federal budget (and based on background interviews with Morrison and Josh Frydenberg): "It will be a budget of pragmatism, not ideology" (23 September); "It is about results and outcomes, not ideological theory or rhetorical inspiration" (26 September); "This budget is the culminating event of the new Liberal order under Morrison-Frydenberg concord and pragmatism" (10 October). When Murphy writes that "Morrison's conservatism is extreme pragmatism in defence of what he regards as the core of the nation," the power-worshipping banality of the press gallery doyen comes easily to mind.

All of this might have come across as defensible, if unedifying, insider journalism, but for the fact that it is so evidently untrue. As numerous alert journalists and commentators have noted, Morrison is a deeply ideological political operator leading a deeply ideological government. This is not only the view of Morrison's opponents on the left. "If anything," a senior government source told Laura Tingle following the Coalition's surprise election victory in 2019, "this government is more ideologically driven than Abbott. They want to win the culture wars they see in education, in the public service, in all of our institutions ... They believe the left has been winning the war for the last twenty years and are determined to turn the tables."

Prophetic as that warning has proven, Murphy seems unconvinced, and more intent on blaming the government's ideological flourishes on its fringe elements, painting Morrison as an innocent victim of their escapades. The man who taunted Labor by smugly brandishing a lump of coal in parliament "couldn't talk about the root cause of the [bushfire] disaster, climate change, because that's quicksand, and the only chance he has of crafting a medium-term solution on that issue is not to talk about it." Apparently Tony Abbott and co. somehow forced climate denial upon the Coalition against its (and Morrison's) will. Meanwhile, universities were deliberately excluded from the JobKeeper scheme because of "a view within *some quarters of the Coalition* that universities are factories of left-wing thought" (my emphasis).

Does anyone seriously believe that these are minority views within the government? They are closer to unimpeachable pillars of Liberal faith. Denial has been the dominant Liberal approach to climate change since the 1990s, i.e. Scott

Morrison's entire career in backroom and parliamentary politics. Does he really deserve to be absolved of blame, or given the benefit of the doubt? Australian universities are presently facing an unprecedented crisis that threatens their very existence, and the Morrison government has not only refused to help, it has inflicted further damage by passing legislation designed to make the humanities and social science degrees it despises unaffordable to the vast majority of potential students. Is this kind of political vandalism just the work of the right-wing fringe, or vindictive and deliberate policy coming from the top?

According to Murphy, Morrison's political missteps are the fault of the right-wing crazies, but when things are going well, such as when the formation of the National Cabinet leads to bipartisan, federal–state cooperation, it is because he is able to "muzzle the more ideological voices inside the Coalition." The false narrative that Murphy has internalised is that Morrison is a more effective version of Malcolm Turnbull, leading a centrist government while managing its reactionary internal pests. The more miserable truth is that, despite the failure of the Dutton putsch in 2018 and the decline of the National Party, the hard right (inclusive of the prime minister) remains in control of the Coalition.

Murphy wants to believe that the pandemic and the government's attendant policy decisions have caused a tectonic shift in Australian politics, whereby government spending will no longer be a dirty concept and the culture wars are relegated to an irrelevant sideshow. She fails to see the wood for the trees. The Morrison government had little choice but to spend big to alleviate the economic harm caused by COVID-19, but, as Richard Cooke observed in *The Monthly* in August, the spending will be "a down payment on future austerity budgets" and the Coalition's ideological and institutional enemies will bear the brunt of the pain. No amount of spin about the prime minister's innate pragmatism can hide these truths.

Dominic Kelly

Damien Freeman

Katharine Murphy begins her essay by explaining that she wants to document what it has been like to be prime minister at a particular moment. She is doing this, she says, partly in order to record and analyse some extraordinary times, but also in order to capture a prime minister "in flight." In the process, she reflects on the nature of pragmatic conservatism, modern leadership, the place of religion in democracy, and, ultimately, the end of certainty. These four ideas deserve to be unpacked a bit more because Murphy's approach to each influences the way she captures this prime minister in flight. A different understanding of these ideas might lead to a somewhat different understanding of the way the prime minister flies.

Murphy understands that Morrison is a conservative leader, and that conservative leaders aim for a form of pragmatism in their policy-making. She advises that "it is helpful to think of Morrison as a project manager rather than the keeper of an ideological flame," and that "he's a doer – not a bard. He wants solutions, not seminars." Morrison told her that JobKeeper and JobSeeker reforms were not about ideology, that "it wasn't a leftie thing. It was the tool needed to do that job. That's why it was done. There was no ideology behind it at all." He is a "nuts-and-bolts political animal, heavy on the party research, light on the Edmund Burke." Murphy concludes that:

> his political philosophy is hard to pin down, because it is predominantly trouble-shooting. By instinct, as we have seen, Morrison is a power player and a populist, not a philosopher; a repairer of walls, not a writer of manifestos. If there's consistency to be found, it's this: Morrison looks for opportunity to show voters he's practical.

As I explain in my book *Abbott's Right: The Conservative Tradition from Menzies to Abbott*, Edmund Burke's conservatives are not ideologically minded. Conservatives have a deep commitment to the shared values of their tradition. To say that they believe in pragmatism does not mean they leave no place for values in their decision-making. It is to say that they have a non-ideological approach to values. It is true that extraordinary circumstances can lead a conservative to rationalise "a cascade of what many regarded as centre-left policy responses" in a way that would be grossly problematic for an ideological liberal. Nothing in this, however, is incompatible with the conservatism of Edmund Burke. Although Burke was critical of the radical change that the French Revolution embodied, he was also critical of the reactionary policies of the *ancien régime*. The Burkean conservative is not afraid of being pragmatic about the kind of change that is required, providing that the policy solutions are proportionate and in keeping with the society's shared values.

Murphy seems to conclude that Morrison's conservatism is extreme pragmatism, rather than pragmatism based on shared values. It is hard to understand how this can be correct. She quotes at length from his maiden speech, in which he cites the shared values to which he is committed, including "loving-kindness, justice and righteousness, to act with compassion and kindness, acknowledging our common humanity, and to consider the welfare of others." The question, then, is whether he has made pragmatic decisions consistent with these values, or whether he has betrayed them. This will require careful analysis because a pragmatic commitment to these shared values might manifest itself in extraordinary ways in extraordinary times.

Murphy also delights in contrasting Morrison with John Howard, who, she writes, "was both pragmatist and ideologue … But Howard had a clear political philosophy which manifested in a policy agenda." Two points need to be kept in mind when thinking about Howard as an ideologue. Yes, he did embrace the ideological approach associated with the New Right, but Murphy cites John Kunkel's observation "that Howard's economic liberalism wasn't pure." At his best, Howard was pragmatic in what he borrowed from the liberal ideologues. Yes, he could be staunchly ideological, and, as Murphy points out, this culminated in his dying "on the hill of WorkChoices, losing his seat in the 2007 election." It did not take conservatives long to concede, however, that this was far from his finest hour. As Tony Abbott explained in his analysis of the Liberal Party's election loss, Howard had become too ideological about industrial relations. The conservative leader was at his best when he adopted a pragmatic, rather than an ideological, approach; when this changed, his political fortunes also changed.

Murphy asks towards the end of her essay, "Will his guiding light be the pragmatism that has been largely on show during the pandemic – a spirit of building and fortifying in the national interest – or will he revert to old, tribal habits if the level of adversity deepens?" That is a fair question. The difficulty is that as circumstances become less dire, it may be that the gap between what seems pragmatic to someone with Morrison's values and what seems pragmatic to the "lefties" he eschews is likely to expand dramatically. The challenge will be for the fair-minded commentator to recognise that his decision-making might still be a product of pragmatism based on values. That said, as Murphy reminds us, the challenge for a genuinely conservative leader is to ensure that pragmatism based on shared values does not give way to the tribal habits that all too easily plague Australian politics.

There are some underlying issues in this essay concerning the nature of democratic leadership in Australia today. In particular, to what extent – and in what ways – should the leader's private life become part of his or her public life? Murphy is convinced that working out what is going on in the private domain of a leader's life is not just important for the political biographer, but also for the political commentator. She suggests that "there is nothing private about a man's hope when the country he leads is suspended between two possibilities." In particular, Murphy dwells on the relevance of Morrison's religious adherence: "Believing in God," she explains, "is a significant part of who Morrison is in his private domain." She wants to investigate the significance of this part of his private life for his public life, but she discovers that "he won't go there." Although he admits to her that "Faith is enormously important to me," he is reluctant to elaborate, telling her only that "I'm uneasy. It always becomes an issue if I talk about it. It is such a personal thing, and no matter how I explain it, it will be misinterpreted."

She notes that in a major speech before the last election, Morrison "promised voters he would 'burn for you every day' if he won the election." Murphy was at the National Press Club when he said this, and reports that "the declaration felt intense." She goes on to explain, however, "In the room, it jarred." She could tell that it was sincere, and that Morrison knew it would resonate with those around the country who understood that "the phrase is invoked in Morrison's religious tradition to signify dedication to a cause." Here is the disconnect between the way that religiously inspired language is received in the National Press Club and in sections of the wider Australian community.

Murphy's essay prompted me to acknowledge another problem. How does an increasingly non-religious Australian population – and commentariat – understand a democratic leader who remains committed to some form of religious conscience? It seems that some commentators had difficulty with the possibility of Tony Abbott's commitment to the Catholic Church intruding into his public life, and yet a different difficulty arises when Scott Morrison declines to discuss the role of his Pentecostal faith in his public life. Democratic leaders will need to engage more seriously with the nature of religious commitment as they, along with Australian society, become less religious.

Murphy introduces the concept of uncertainty at the end of the essay when she asks, "Can we go on being stoic when anxiety and uncertainty has no end date? Do we have the collective fortitude to live in uncertainty without turning on each other, without hunting scapegoats?" The end of certainty is more than a passing reference in this essay; Murphy chooses it for her title. In the context of Australian political commentary, this title references Paul Kelly's monumental tome of the same name.

As Kelly points out, political leadership in the 1980s saw Bob Hawke and Paul Keating embrace policies that would have been anathema to Labor politicians for generations. It also involved John Howard leading an opposition that supported the dismantling of Australian Settlement policies. The uncertainty in 2020 is not the same as the uncertainty of the 1980s, but it is wise to remember that coping with uncertainty – indeed the seeming end of certainty – is a constant in politics. That does not diminish the crisis of the moment that Murphy captures, but it does help us to gain some perspective on it.

Murphy concludes that "it's hard to get a fix on" Scott Morrison and admits that she finds him "confounding in a number of respects." Morrison may well be confounding, but part of Murphy's uncertainty might have to do with the categories she recruits in her political commentary. Conservative leaders have a particular understanding of pragmatism based on shared values, the nature of leadership, and the relationship between religion and public life. Scott Morrison's prime ministership may or may not exemplify the best of conservative leadership in public life, and it is right that political commentators should scrutinise it. It is also right, however, that progressive commentators should understand the conservative approach to public life before making judgments about the success of conservative leaders, or the desirability of conservative leadership in public life at all.

Damien Freeman

James Walter

A crisis is always both a challenge and an opportunity: an opportunity not only for a leader to demonstrate capacity, but also for an astute observer to capture, as Katharine Murphy puts it, "a prime minister in flight, at a critical moment." Since Murphy has become a go-to commentator on and analyst of contemporary politics, adept at illuminating individual qualities, it is an enticing proposition. I've always relished Murphy's wonderful encapsulation of Peta Credlin as she departed mainstream politics, "refusing to shrink, rolling on, stoking her own mythology like a little sustaining campfire, owning a persona she invented for a purpose, refusing to defer."

Her subject this time is Scott Morrison, about whom she has already written extensively. Will pandemic politics provide the summative moment in which she can now capture the Morrison persona, showing it to be "invented for a purpose," and explain what it presages for meeting the crisis we confront?

First, the nature of the challenge. The essay title encourages one to accept the supposition that this is a moment of unprecedented uncertainty. While that is uncontested, it might also be said that the pandemic has laid bare the untenable costs of the risk society that has long been with us.

Over recent decades, both Coalition and Labor governments have progressively shifted risk from the state to individuals. They privatised public services where possible (for example, energy services), contracted out "client services" to private providers (witness JobSeeker and aged care), "marketised" higher education while diminishing public funding and withdrew support for social housing, to name a few instances. They relied on regulatory oversight rather than direct engagement to ensure the public good. Citizens were expected to be capable of informed decisions in a context where they had now to deal with commercial entities rather than accountable public institutions. Morrison and his colleagues have, until now, been fervent exponents of this paradigm.

Polls have shown for near twenty years how unhappy the public is with this process. Yet since the major parties were complicit in the transition, electoral options for change were limited. Now the pandemic has starkly exposed costs that were evident well before it arrived: inadequate regulation, the precariousness of gig employment, the sapping of consumer confidence in the face of wage stagnation as "markets" privilege profit and shareholder returns above workers, the disadvantaged being treated as problems demanding case management rather than as casualties of circumstances beyond their control, homelessness and, in Murphy's words, "the terrible indignity of ageing, high levels of youth unemployment, the fragility of a world-class university sector."

How did the Morrison Coalition government respond? It recognised that in most cases (apart from that of the universities), these costs could not, for the moment, be ignored. The vulnerable homeless are a threat to public health and must be housed. Unemployment (and casualisation) must be addressed by keeping people connected to the labour market lest the demand for benefits overwhelm the system. Business and unions must find common ground. Consumption had to be maintained, both to shore up businesses and to sustain aggregate demand. Private health providers must work with public hospitals. And many restraints on freedom of movement must be introduced to halt transmission of the virus.

The Coalition listened to health experts on flattening the curve of infection and, in adopting means to stabilise consumption and demand, responded to the advice of a public service of which it had long been sceptical. The government also realised the importance of national, cross-party teams by engaging with state leaders, sought to establish common purpose between business and unions – and avoided mimicking the approach of allies in the United States and the United Kingdom, whose management of the crisis has proved disastrous. In many respects, it reversed approaches thought integral to the Coalition DNA.

Many have commented on these remarkable changes, but Murphy is especially good at outlining the stages and timelines of development as seen by insiders, and by Morrison himself. Was it, then, a new beginning, driven by a pragmatic, "shape-shifting" leader who was growing in the job, capable of adapting to radical change and bringing his party with him? Murphy would like to think so: a recurrent theme in her argument is that of a leader learning from experience, of Morrison watching others and reading the room for what is needed, of a pragmatist who is "protean" and hard to get a fix on. "This guy," she remarks, "can be anything he thinks he needs to be." She leaves us with that image of mutability: "He hasn't landed yet ... He's still journeying to the core of his own project."

This is not entirely persuasive. One can read the evidence Murphy so usefully presents as confirming persistent elements of Morrison's operational mode. The habit of giving away as little as possible, telling only what he wants to convey rather than engaging with an inquiry, was captured by many commentators, including Murphy, before the 2019 election. Here, she remarks that in agreeing to an interview, "Morrison's objective is not to be understood ... So don't expect much sharing," and refers to his preferred method of communicating via a circle of broadcasting "mates."

It is an approach that accords with the carefully crafted ScoMo persona, the "daggy Dad" whose very ordinariness suggests that he understands your interests without having to go on about things. This too was a persona invented for a purpose. It served well to shield him from questions and to obscure the calculating politician in delivering the "Morrison Miracle" election victory of 2019. Now it implies the caring dad, responsible for the health of the nation. Of course, every politician wants to manage their image, but Morrison's preoccupation with control, screening any intrusion, is what seems to make him hard to read. Yet there are telling indicators, which Murphy captures, even while resisting certain conclusions.

She demonstrates effectively that Morrison is a power politician, not a persuader, a man who "isn't well liked in politics. He plays to win." But then she remarks that it is hard to identify any abiding objectives, asking, "What hill would Scott Morrison die on?"

Unlike Murphy, but drawing on the evidence she presents, I suggest the answer is twofold: an artful connection of power politics with religious conviction. Morrison makes no secret of his faith, but implies it is private, not a political issue. One can accept, as Murphy does, that Morrison's faith is significant. How, though, is one to reconcile his commitment to the teachings of Jesus with the lack of compassion in so many of the policies for which he has been responsible? Morrison would not be the first believer to consult his conscience about such quandaries, only to find that his political instincts were right (Alfred Deakin springs to mind). The particularity of his commitment, however, is key: he is, as a politician, consistently reading the room, but he is, as a believer, also "sizing up which side you are on," with, as he expressed it in his maiden speech, recognition of "an unchanging and absolute standard of what is good and what is evil."

If you are not "one of us," therefore, expect no mercy: it is a recipe for reversion to partisan intensification. Further, this religious sensibility can accommodate the methods of the power politician without hypocrisy. The man who, to paraphrase pioneering political psychologist Harold Lasswell, steers by power chances, now has an added benefit: he has God on his side. He will die on a hill that he determines, after prayer, is "right." But however he persuades himself and rationalises it for others, it will be about fighting to maintain power. It is not a matter of adherence to specific principles: he can dismiss the mantras of some colleagues as "boring, tired, tedious and claustrophobic," and appear to be the fixer and project manager, pursuing "non-ideological conservatism," but it may be a mistake to forget the ruthlessness incipient in such righteousness.

Morrison is not so deluded as to think he can do what is needed alone – this is the limitation on what Murphy calls "trying on the Trump suit." He recognises he needs others: experts, public servants and, in current circumstances, the state leaders. Yet here, too, is a power chance – a deliberative mode that "makes the upper echelons of the government drill concepts into submission," and the creation of a leadership team, in the National Cabinet, that dispensed with staff and officials, became more important for a time than his own cabinet, muzzled the more ideological voices inside the Coalition and rendered his Coalition partner, the National Party, "a total irrelevance." Now, in the National Cabinet, which is expected to continue, he has a top-down instrument, largely free of parliamentary scrutiny and remote from officialdom. Surely this is an accentuation of executive power of which Murphy might have said more?

Of course, Morrison did not have it all his own way in negotiating with other strong leaders and dealing with the capacity of states prepared to go their own way. Yet circumstances allowed him continually to assert that he spoke for the nation, while others who would not comply were endangering the national interest. As tensions and disagreements accumulated, it was all too easy to revert to partisan targeting of supposed miscreants – such as Daniel Andrews (in which the Murdoch press provided him robust support). If, as Murphy suggests, he can be "anything he thinks he needs to be," why was he not able to be a team builder when this was needed? Because he is not a persuader and has always played to win.

And so here we are again. The opportunities that so many saw as inherent in the crisis management of the pandemic to shift the national conversation away from the dead ends of the past decade, to address the untenable costs rendered so clear by its arrival, are in danger of being frittered away. The helping hand extended to the most disadvantaged has a sunset clause: social housing, for instance, will not be a priority; the gig economy will not be addressed. Tax cuts return to the top of the agenda, despite a majority of economists arguing that other forms of stimulus would be more effective. Tim Colebatch and Ross Gittins remark that the 2020 budget rejects the advice of economists in favour of boosting support to key Liberal Party constituencies: business and middle- to upper-middle-income earners. Culture wars are cranked up again as universities become a particular target for intervention and diminution. The public sector, so essential in managing the crisis, is again to be relegated: private-sector leadership is to be our salvation. The opportunity to encourage investment in renewables and storage in building a more reliable and cost-efficient energy sector is forsaken as gas-led recovery is mooted as integral to industrial revival and new infrastructure development. Peter Hartcher has commented: "After a couple of years of extraordinary short-term measures, the government, post-pandemic, plans to go back to essentially the same program it had pre-pandemic."

Does Morrison look like a shape-shifter now, capable of forging a new way forward and carrying his party, and the country, with him? Or are we seeing a reversion to tribal habits, a default to familiar settings that were inadequate even before the crisis from which we are yet to emerge? It looks like the same ScoMo to me.

James Walter

Lesley Russell

Katharine Murphy's essay on Scott Morrison and pandemic politics is the first of likely many to explore how Australia's government leaders have responded and continue to respond to the coronavirus pandemic and its associated impacts.

Her findings must be regarded as interim, with the long-term health, economic, social and international security consequences of this new viral foe yet to be fully demonstrated and understood.

Just as there is no recognised playbook for how to respond to this new pandemic, neither is there an agreed yardstick for measuring the success of the response. The most obvious questions to ask are:

Has Australia followed the best, most up-to-date scientific advice and evidence?

Has Australia done better than other, similar countries?

Have fewer people died in Australia than elsewhere?

Has the economy been less adversely affected?

There are factual answers to these questions; for example, a recently published analysis finds that if Australia had gone down the same path as England and Wales in March and April, there would have been 16,000 more deaths. In contrast to the United States, where First Nations people have been disproportionately affected by COVID-19, Indigenous Australians are significantly under-represented in the nation's cases despite a higher-risk status.

These answers cast Australia in a positive light, but they must also be seen in the context of ethics and fairness:

What has been the impact on peoples' trust in government and support for government decisions?

Have there been disproportionate impacts on some population groups?

Is there community empathy and support for those who have suffered the most?

Have government resources and taxpayers' dollars been used effectively?

On balance, with the second wave of the pandemic seemingly under control but so many unknowns ahead, Australia has done well. Yes, there have been mistakes made, some of them serious and – in retrospect – unnecessary. The extent to which Morrison can claim credit for the positives and be blamed for the negatives is up for discussion.

As the essay points out, the pragmatic, rational, science-based approach of the prime minister and his advisers meant that Australia has not gone down the disastrous paths of the United States, the United Kingdom and parts of Europe. The early warning signals from these countries were duly noted and acted upon in ways that – for the most part – were timely, appropriate and encompassed the whole population.

Australia faced the epidemic with some inherent advantages, including high-functioning health-care and public health systems which, together with the health-care workforce, were capable of the needed expansion and flexibility to deal with the pandemic; the ability to close international borders; and community and government trust in an excellent national cadre of scientific and medical experts that generally meant a willingness to follow official advice and directives.

These were boosted by the nationwide, bipartisan approach from governments, the ready and free availability of testing and the necessary tracing and follow-up efforts, and, most particularly, the financial and employment supports that are essential corollaries of lockdown, business disruption and social isolation.

The essay's findings make it clear that Morrison's early leadership on the pandemic response was based as much on his need to atone for his failures during the bushfires as it was on his self-described "fixer" approach to governing. He established the National Cabinet arrangement as a way to project himself into the centre of crisis management and appear in control, although it also facilitated cooperative action and the best use of the available federal levers. And his concerns have always been more about the economic and market consequences of the pandemic than the costs to society and the emotional toll on individuals and communities.

However, the nation was the beneficiary of his ability to wrangle strong-minded premiers with their own agendas (at least this was the case early on), the willingness of all heads of government to listen to and act on the expert advice they received, and the fact that the conservative coalition Morrison leads was willing (at least temporarily) to change its political stance and deliver a "non-ideological conservative" financial response to the pandemic.

(As an aside, it's interesting to speculate on the role of Treasury Secretary Steven Kennedy in the economic response. He was uniquely qualified for this advisory role, having been a nurse before he switched to economics and having conducted research on the economic impact of a pandemic.)

The hard work of government leaders and the health-care workforce and the sacrifices of working Australians and their families have brought us to what is hopefully the end of the second wave of the pandemic. Meanwhile the United States and the United Kingdom seem to be headed into a third wave, a situation aggravated by the arrival of winter and irrational leadership from President Donald Trump and Prime Minister Boris Johnson (leadership informed neither by science nor even by their own personal experiences of infection).

Most Australians look on askance. Surely some self-congratulations are in order? Perhaps, but as the coronavirus pandemic moves from an acute national disaster to a chronic policy dilemma, pre-existing problems remain and new ones loom. Morrison says he likes problem-solving – but now the problems are difficult and expensive, requiring long-term vision and sustained commitment.

As it has everywhere, the pandemic in this country has exposed the weaknesses in social welfare and health-care systems, and socio-economic inequalities, and threatened the inclusiveness of a multicultural society. Too many Australians and people resident in Australia have not received needed financial assistance, frontline workers have been deprived of necessary personal protective equipment and support for their physical and mental wellbeing, communication with culturally and linguistically diverse communities has been poor, and vulnerable people in aged and disability care have died because of failures of staffing and infection control. The burdens have been doubly imposed on those still reeling from the summer bushfires.

It seems Morrison now has little interest in understanding or addressing these issues. He is not the uniter-in-chief; there is no longer any attempt to convey a national unity approach from National Cabinet. He is happy to play state premiers off against each other and second-guess their decisions. The federal government refuses to accept responsibly for the aged-care catastrophe, and there is an almost punitive approach to certain population groups needing help.

Morrison has made a series of significant coronavirus funding announcements, but much of the funding is yet to flow where it is needed. Moreover, although the exigencies of the pandemic have highlighted new ways of working, educating and delivering health care, Morrison and his cabinet have shown no interest in promulgating reforms.

This is exemplified in the 2020–21 federal budget. With its focus squarely on the economy and jobs, this is not a reforming budget, it is not a "build back better" budget (to borrow from Jacinda Ardern and Joe Biden). Former treasury secretary Ken Henry was quoted as saying, "They've delivered a stimulus budget. Which is fine, but they haven't delivered reform."

There has undoubtedly been a significant financial commitment to addressing the immediate impact of the pandemic and rebuilding the economy – total emergency spending now amounts to $397 billion – but this is insufficient for the greater need. The JobSeeker coronavirus supplement has been extended to March – at a reduced rate – and beyond that may revert to a rate that makes paying for essentials such as food and medicine a struggle. Failure to properly subsidise child care affects the career prospects of many women. There is nothing to boost employment opportunities for older women.

There is nothing here to tackle the reforms in public health and health-care delivery, workforce and financing that will be so necessary to address the expected burdens of "long COVID" (the manifold, long-term consequences of the infection), the burgeoning rate of mental health disorders, and the mounting problems caused by delayed access to cancer screening, effective management of chronic conditions and growing waiting lists for elective surgery. Not to mention the preparations that should begin now for the next pandemic that will surely arrive.

The government chose not to react to the Productivity Commission's report on its mental health inquiry (which it is yet to release) and the interim reports from the Royal Commission into Aged Care Quality and Safety. Reforms have been urgently needed in both these areas for decades and the pandemic has magnified this. There was nothing to tackle social housing needs and homelessness. At a time when the value of academic expertise, analysis and research is highlighted daily, Morrison and his cabinet have instituted changes to the university sector that will see thousands of jobs lost, teaching standards decline and funds for research dry up.

The coronavirus pandemic has brought the complexity of policy-making in the context of scientific uncertainty into sharp focus. Communication and decision-making in such exceptional times require courage, clear thinking, consultation and humility. The complexity cannot be made to disappear with a surfeit of confidence; neither is procrastination an option. Policy must change as new evidence and data are generated and the cases for such changes must be effectively made to all stakeholders.

On my analysis, based on Katharine Murphy's excellent essay and Morrison's subsequent actions, Morrison gets a pass grade for the initial months of the pandemic response, but he has failed to sustain this and has reverted to his true form – more partisan, more narrowly focused and much less visionary than the country needs or deserves.

Lesley Russell

Celeste Liddle

I'm writing this response to Katharine Murphy's essay *The End of Certainty* the same day that the Victorian premier, Daniel Andrews, has announced what is effectively an end to the Melbourne lockdown. In mere minutes, for the first time since June, I will be able to see my parents, two of my siblings and one of my nephews, in a space where all of our new 25-kilometre radii overlap. Although I am just weeks away from completing my Masters, I may actually get to set foot on campus. In three weeks, my partner and I may be able to celebrate our anniversary at the very pub we met at. We've been in each other's hair for seven months straight, but despite this, we still very much feel like celebrating us. Yet to be honest, it feels surreal, like I need to see it happen to believe it, because if I have learnt anything this year, it's that situations can change so quickly. A healthy degree of cynicism is not just wise, it's essential.

Murphy's essay has provided us with invaluable insight into Scott Morrison and his government's responses up until August; perhaps this comment will be more of a postscript to things she foreshadowed in the closing chapters – the tension between Morrison and Andrews, for example, as the second wave took hold in Victoria. And nationalism – why it seemed more important in a global pandemic and how it was manifesting.

I can't help but feel let down by our political leadership. This pandemic and the formation of the National Cabinet could have led to some of Australia's finest moments – it certainly provided opportunities for cohesion and growth – yet I don't think this has been the case. I'm not an expert. I'm not an epidemiologist, nor a forensic pathologist. I'm a mere commentator rather than a journalist, and my COVID "comfort spending" credit card bill attests that I am definitely not an economist. I do, however, possess a keenly trained eye when it comes to social policy and political leadership. Despite this, Murphy reminded me of why I felt so incredibly confused back in March, when all of a sudden we were locked down. Political leaders had failed to inform the public properly about the threat of this terrible virus, and I myself made comparisons to the flu based on what I'd heard. Indeed, while videos circulated on social media of supermarket shoppers fighting over toilet paper and canned tomatoes, most of us sat back and laughed at people we deemed "doomsday prepper fools."

Perhaps it is the progressive Melbourne bubble I live in, but at the beginning, the Morrison–Andrews situation felt very much like an interplay between a middle-aged white man viewed as an incompetent national leader and another middle-aged white man viewed as a competent state leader. Many Victorians saw the Andrews government's moves for stronger early containment measures as a sign of strength. So, sadly, we said a temporary goodbye to our live venues, our pubs, our restaurants, our cultural scene, our sporting scene (even though these are the things we like to wave smugly in the faces of other Australian capitals) for the greater good.

Likewise, although Murphy is completely correct in highlighting just how unprecedented it was for a Liberal government to vastly increase welfare payments, I think many in Victoria saw the horrifically long queues at Centrelink and viewed the increase as long overdue. Probably more notable was that the Victorian government appeared to be looking after those the federal government had forgotten. Homeless people, for example, being housed in hotels, or the emergency payments made to international university students who'd been left without support and not much more from Morrison than a "go home." It was rough, but we flattened the curve, rejoiced and then headed back to our (now completely seated and spaced-out) pubs for a celebratory pint.

It clearly didn't last. In July I seized the opportunity to go to country Victoria for a break and just as we were leaving, the postcode lockdown and housing commission tower detention began. By the time I got back, all of Melbourne had plunged into Stage 3 restrictions, and Stage 4 followed weeks later. And here begins my criticism of the Andrews approach, but the writing had actually been on the wall several months earlier and I had failed to note it. Back in April, it had been reported that the majority of non-compliance fines for lockdowns were not being issued in the wealthy suburbs such as Toorak, whose residents were bringing the virus home with them from their international skiing trips. The fines were being issued in working-class outer areas with a higher proportion of migrant communities, and unfortunately, this divide between rich and poor, white and brown and black, continued. Perhaps what Murphy observed about government use of "nationalism" has even morphed into "Victorianism" (for want of a better term) at times.

The Andrews government was not responsible for the attacks on Asian students in February and March, when unthinking people read memes on the internet and set out to blame anyone they believed looked remotely Chinese: Australia remains a deeply racist country, shaped both by the fiction of *terra nullius* and its old friend the White Australia Policy. The Andrews government did, however, play a role in the demonisation of the Black Lives Matter rally in June. This is not just because a "senior government source" leaked a fake report to *The Age* that attendees planned to spit on police, but also because, despite all the efforts the diligent organisers made to work with community health organisations, provide personal protective equipment to attendees and ensure that messages of distancing were repeated throughout the protest, they were still slapped with large fines. Not a single case of COVID community transmission was recorded due to the rally, yet the waters were so muddied by the government and their police service that many ordinary Victorians came to believe it was the cause of the second wave.

When it became abundantly clear the rally had not caused the second wave, government messaging seemed to focus on families having "large gatherings." This was taken by some as a dog whistle allowing racists to blame ethnic families or Eid celebrations. The ground-work had been done to ensure mainstream society would give the required hegemonic assent to the lockdown of multicultural postcodes and commission towers, which housed a high proportion of impoverished migrants. The baddies were those "other people" and it was for Victoria's own good that police were guarding their every move.

What we weren't aware of then was that the government knew where the second wave had come from, and it wasn't those "other people." It was its own quarantine program. Findings of the commission into the quarantine program are due to be handed down soon, but we already know this: that the government elected to use private security guards, even though publicly funded options were available (for example, the police or Army Reserve); that the three companies it contracted the security to then sub-contracted out to other companies, which then contracted out further until some security guards were engaged via WhatsApp messages; that, notwithstanding reports in certain publications regarding security guards engaging in sex with guests, the first person infected was a hotel duty manager; that the infection spread from low-paid, insecure workers in one industry to low-paid, insecure workers in other industries, such as meatworks, aged care and factories. Eighty per cent of second-wave transmissions were happening in the workplace.

This was when the government script flipped from blaming "others" to "individuals." Regardless of sentiments expressed at the daily press conferences, I've never felt we were "all in it together." The quarantine outbreak and the infection chain that followed exposed deep systemic problems, but the key messaging at the press conferences was about "individual responsibility." Sure, government directives on masks, restricting contact and movement, and getting tested even with the smallest of symptoms were prudent health policy. But when I heard that fines for "breaking curfew" – a government measure based purely on easier policing that had not been recommended by the Chief Health Officer or the Police Commissioner – had been worn disproportionately by Sudanese and Aboriginal people, or that residents in the locked-down commission towers and poorer, multicultural postcodes were forced to translate health directives for themselves with the assistance of NGOs, the sentiment of all being in it together seemed rather hollow. The towers were locked down with four hours' notice and the "detention" measures were criticised in a scathing letter from the UN's former special rapporteur on adequate housing.

What's more, social media has been a particularly vicious place to "live" during lockdown. When I wasn't seeing blatantly racist materials blaming Black Lives Matter for the second wave or comparing the premier to everyone from Mao to Hitler, I was setting my clock by the daily chants of #IStandWithDan as people reacted to criticism of the government from the right-wing press. An online cult of personality grew up around Andrews, with journalists demonised who directed tricky questions his way. When quality publications such as The Saturday Paper, The Guardian and The Age are publishing valid criticism and sections of the left on social media are treating it all as an affront requiring punishment of the journalists, I have real concerns for open and honest political dialogue.

COVID is going nowhere fast. The Andrews government knows this and has a plan leading to Victorians living a "COVID-normal" life. We're in this until a vaccine is developed or the virus dies out, as SARS did – whatever comes first. In a recent opinion piece, Virginia Trioli put the question to the Victorian government: "Victorians have done our bit to suppress COVID. Premier, have you done yours?" She asked whether the Department of Health and Human Services had been bolstered, whether more contact tracers had been engaged, whether "infection protocols" had been strengthened and supported in high-risk areas such as hospitals, aged care and meatworks. I want to know all this too. The toll of the second wave on Victorians, particularly Melburnians, has been immense – economically, socially, physically, mentally and mortality-wise. We don't want to end up here again.

Considering all this, the most striking takeaway from Murphy's essay is that this tale of Australian political leadership is "to be continued." For me it's been an educational journey – I now know a lot more about a conservative prime minister in whom I'd previously shown little interest. I have indeed, at times, been surprised by his pragmatism and innovation while still gnashing my teeth at federal failures. Similarly, though, I have watched a much-admired Labor premier be punitive, fuel fear and division and be buffered in these problematic tactics by sections of the community who should know better. I want to be clear here: I am not saying I have not supported the Victorian leadership at times. I am saying that if we end up in this situation again and we do truly want to be "all in it together," then we must be more critical and call for more accountability. We must be able to trust that our elected leaders, whether federal, state or in the form of a National Cabinet, are speaking to each other, that the various ministries collaborate and that they make the right decisions for the entire community, particularly supporting those who need help most. Simple hashtags deifying leadership while demonising reporters just ain't going to cut it.

Celeste Liddle

Hugh Mackay

We have always known that Katharine Murphy is in the front rank of political journalists, and that we are fortunate to have her in our midst, especially at a time like this: her account of the political response to COVID-19 is documentary journalism at its best. But *The End of Certainty* demonstrates that Murphy is also a formidable essayist. The broad sweep of this essay, and the sheer quality of the writing, set it apart as one of the finest recent examples of the form. I'm not surprised she chose a quote from Gerard Manley Hopkins early on: there are many flashes of her own writing that could have been inspired by Hopkins – including her fondness for using compounds like "war-game" and "blame-shift" as verbs.

This response will focus on two aspects of the essay: the personality of the prime minister, and the social impact of the pandemic.

Murphy has presented us with some acute observations of Scott Morrison the man. Given her limited access, and the guarded nature of some of Morrison's responses, her insights and interpretations are impressive, and shed light on some aspects of Morrison's behaviour whose significance we might otherwise not grasp. For example, her assessment of him as "project manager" rather than a political philosopher or policy-maker may account for his apparent insensitivity to some of the demands of the prime ministerial role, most notably in the bushfire crisis, but also in the early stumbles in his handling of the pandemic.

His irritability is worth knowing about, and his impatience with parliament itself helps to explain his preference for "mates radio" over Question Time, and for wandering around in a baseball cap and high-vis vest over parliamentary debates or robust press conferences. The sight of him scrolling through his phone while Anthony Albanese delivered his budget reply speech on 8 October looked like a sign of contempt for the institution, not just for the leader of the Opposition. (Josh Frydenberg, by contrast, appeared to give Albanese appropriately courteous attention.)

Murphy assures us that Morrison is adaptable and a quick learner, but it's odd to think we might have a prime minister who isn't comfortable in the parliament – the most potent symbol of our democracy.

"Scotty from marketing" is a sobriquet Morrison obviously hates, but there's a good aspect to it: his marketing background has taught him to respect the views of his market and to see his political challenge not as winning the voters to his side, but convincing them that he's on *their* side – the classic position of successful brand marketing: "It's not about you responding to us; it's about us responding to you." His assessment of the mood of the electorate, as reported by Murphy, is spot-on. The unanswerable question is whether his pandemic lessons – more patience, more empathy, more sensitivity, more respect for experts (including climate scientists) – will survive the COVID era and translate into a permanent shift. If it does, he could be in the job for years to come.

The big shift in politics during the pandemic has been the nation's willingness – even eagerness – for governments to play a bigger part in our lives; to tell us what to do; to *lead*, in other words, and perhaps even to inspire (certainly to reassure). In spite of our much-vaunted larrikinism, we are actually a rather acquiescent society compared with many others – most notably the United States; obedience comes easily to us. But we had certainly become disenchanted with politics before the pandemic arrived, and it's worth asking why that was. (It wasn't only politics we were disenchanted with, of course: also banks, churches, mass media, trade unions ... it's been a rough time for institutions, in terms of public respect and trust.)

We become disenchanted with institutions when we feel as if they've lost sight of their reason for being: to serve the society that brought them into being or gave them their social licence to operate. We learn to distrust them when we think they are most concerned with serving their own ends – particularly when they are preoccupied with their own power plays – and that's been a big criticism of Australian politics for many years.

During the pandemic, it seemed that governments – especially state governments – were unambiguously attuned to the wellbeing of the community. And so, against the trend, our trust rose. It will only continue to rise if politicians, including Morrison, understand why we have parliaments in the first place. Perhaps his irritation with parliament and its rituals and procedures means he hasn't yet fully grasped that it's our institution, not his: lack of respect for the institution feels like lack of respect for us.

One other thing about Morrison intrigued Murphy: his religious faith. She is clearly sympathetic, as most Australians are. (I've reported elsewhere on the phenomenon of "faith envy.") When Morrison says that Australia "is not a secular country," he's right: the last Census showed that almost two-thirds of Australians identify with a religion, including 52 per cent who still identify as Christian. The thing that interests many Australians is not that Morrison has a religious faith, but what kind of faith it is. Though Pentecostalism is the fastest-growing branch of Christianity here and around the world, knowledge of its doctrines is limited and awareness is mostly focused on practices such as "speaking in tongues," ecstatic swooning, arm raising, and enthusiastic singing of rock-gospel songs.

The thing that caught my attention in Murphy's discussion of Morrison's faith was her sense that he is doubt-free, and that's a worry. Doubt, after all, is faith's oxygen: if we knew, we wouldn't need to believe. It's arguable that faith not washed by tides of doubt is not faith at all. What sometimes passes for faith might be an embrace of dogma, doctrine or prejudice; it might be a strong connection to a faith community, or trust in a religious institution; it might be more about values than beliefs; it might be a commitment to certain practices that bring comfort; but is it "faith"?

Given that this is supposed to be such a central part of Morrison's life, it's not surprising that many of us are curious to know what kind of belief system he has. Does he, for instance, believe in an interventionist supreme being who could actually be bothered delivering a "miraculous" election victory to someone in a small country at the bottom of the world, perhaps because he prayed so hard for it? Does he pray for rain, as if there's a God who acts as controller-in-chief of the weather, turning the tap on or off according to the quantity and quality of human requests to do so?

Does he share the literal belief of many Pentecostalists — though of very few other Christians — in The Rapture (a fast-approaching end-of-time event when Christian believers, both dead and alive, would rise bodily from the earth "to meet the Lord in the air")? And if so, does that make him more fatalistic and less interested in long-range planning, especially in response to climate change? The answer to such questions could be highly relevant to Morrison's approach to politics, and to fossil fuels. Perhaps it's no wonder he ducked the issue of religion when Murphy raised it.

The social effects of the pandemic were lightly touched on by Murphy, yet she seemed reluctant to accept that her reflections on her own experience — of a rejuvenated sense of neighbourhood, in particular — might be more than a surrender to sentimentality. In fact, Murphy's experience reflected not only what has happened here, and around the world, in response to the pandemic, but also what usually happens to human communities in a crisis.

The first reaction is often unformed and exaggerated fear, leading to panic and outbreaks of selfish behaviour. But nobler responses usually prevail, simply because we know we are members of a social species that can only survive – let alone thrive – to the extent that we acknowledge that we indivisibly belong to each other, bear some responsibility for each other's wellbeing, and depend upon each other. Murphy's experience of regularly waving to a neighbour she had not previously acknowledged was one tiny sign of a more general COVID-led trend: not only is government back in our lives; so is the neighbourhood. Perhaps our little taste of social isolation has brought home to us what it must feel like for those who are permanently at risk of feeling left out, such as older people living alone, single parents, people with a disability or those struggling with mental illness.

Early in the course of the pandemic, I encountered two young men via a webinar, who were both new to their neighbourhoods – one in Melbourne, one in Sydney. Both were living alone. In both cases, early in the lockdown, they put notes in the letterboxes of all the houses in their street, offering to help out with shopping or other chores. Their deeply human instinct was to connect.

Zoom, and an ever-growing family of similar platforms, quickly emerged as a way to "connect" for people deprived of social contact. The age of video meetings, online parties, webinars and "virtual" events of all kinds was suddenly upon us. Zoom and its siblings seemed like the techno-saviours we needed, until we discovered – *surprise, surprise* – that, just like social media posts, Zoom-type links run a distant second to the real thing; better than nothing, but lacking the crucial ingredients for social connection: eye-contact and actual, physical presence. While the technology gave us a brilliant stop-gap, it also served as a persuasive reminder that "connected but lonely" is a perfectly possible situation: lots of messaging, but no *presence*.

As Murphy's quote from Jodie McVernon of the Doherty Institute put it: "The social measures we are taking also have health impacts." Chief among those impacts are the health hazards that arise from widespread social isolation increasing the incidence of loneliness. It's not only anxiety and depression that are likely to increase in response to social isolation: there's also an increased risk of hypertension, inflammation, cognitive decline and addiction. That's why psychologists are now saying that social isolation is a greater risk to public health than obesity. The federal government's increased attention to the mental health consequences of the pandemic is therefore welcome.

Another positive human instinct on display was our willingness to accept the restrictions on our individual lives in the interests of the common good. We all have the capacity to show compassion, kindness and respect towards each other – even towards total strangers – and when there's a crisis, that tendency is far more evident than the reckless individualism of a minority of citizens.

Murphy correctly points out that one effect of the pandemic is to expose our vulnerabilities as a society. The question is whether the pandemic will jolt us into a more compassionate response to homelessness, for instance, or to the destructive shift in the labour market towards insecure employment. At least any stigma attached to unemployment has now been washed away, but we are still remarkably reluctant to acknowledge that, even when things return to "normal," we simply don't have enough work for everyone who wants to work.

We've been here before, of course. The Great Depression was a dreadful period for our parents or grandparents to live through, yet they looked back on it with a kind of gratitude: it was a time when their values were forged in hardship, and their priorities were clarified. Counterintuitively, many of them described themselves as "lucky" for having been tempered by such adversity, and they typically claimed that the lessons of the Depression never left them.

This points to the only two aspects of Murphy's essay where I beg to differ. When she says that "crises are tipping points where societies are consumed by the worst of their collective impulses" and refers to our "unmoored humanity," I find myself rushing to the defence of humankind, based on such evidence as Murphy's experience in her own street. Crises are, more typically, episodes from which we learn important lessons about what it means to be human and how best to preserve social cohesion in the face of catastrophe. Communities affected by this year's bushfires certainly didn't report an outbreak of bad behaviour; quite the reverse.

It's the same for individuals who deal with personal trauma – relationship breakdown, serious illness, retrenchment, bereavement. The typical (though not universal) response is to look back on such events as times when we faced questions like these: "What really matters?" "Am I living the kind of life I really want to live?" "Am I being true to the values I claim to espouse?" Adversity is often the trigger for self-discovery, and the pandemic certainly provided plenty of opportunities for self-examination.

One obvious social consequence of all this disruption and introspection is that many of us are determined to restructure our lives; to be more flexible about our working arrangements; to cut back on pointless busyness and the stress it induces; to be less inclined to rush hither and thither; to rethink travel plans; to value home and family – and neighbourhood – more than we did.

The other point of difference: I suspect that Murphy somewhat overestimates the scale of COVID-19's impact on Australia. Every avoidable death is a tragedy;

the economic costs are huge – but let's keep it in perspective. At the time of writing, we had had about 900 COVID deaths out of a population of 25 million. The Spanish flu of 1919 killed about 15,000 Australians out of a population of 5 million – mainly because we didn't then know what we now know about infection control. World War I caused about 60,000 Australian deaths, and another 26,000 Australian lives were lost in World War II. Unemployment was far worse, in scale and consequences, in the Great Depression than now – and social security provisions were even less generous.

By contrast with those cataclysmic events, and thanks to radical countermeasures, the pandemic's direct impact has been mild, even though its social and political consequences could turn out to be far-reaching. Of course, it *seems* so much worse because, thanks to our famous twenty-eight consecutive years of economic growth, we had been lulled into a state of dreamy complacency, as if we could always rely on our luck to keep us out of trouble.

Finally, the essay's title, *The End of Certainty*. It might have been borrowed from Paul Kelly's seminal book of 1992, or perhaps drawn from the conclusion of Jodie McVernon's quote: "The dilemmas are very real. There are no guarantees. There is no certainty." But, as I read it, McVernon was not suggesting that COVID-19 marked the end of some mythical period of certainty. Rather, it was another reminder that, when it comes to human affairs – biological, psychological, political, social, economic or cultural – nothing is ever certain. The pandemic hasn't ended certainty for us, but perhaps it has reminded us, as crises and catastrophes always do, that the very idea of certainty is a seductive delusion.

Hugh Mackay

Katharine Murphy

Both a lifetime ago, and only a few months past, I interviewed Scott Morrison in what turned out to be the last hours before he and Daniel Andrews understood there would be a substantial second wave of COVID-19 infections in Victoria. The writer in me appreciates this bit of symmetry. Victoria went into lockdown as I was finalising the Quarterly Essay, and then the state reopened as I crafted this response to the thoughtful and generous feedback you've enjoyed in the preceding pages. But it feels cretinous to be musing about symmetry in 2020, when people have suffered.

Australia has fared significantly better than elsewhere in the plague of 2020, largely because of the values our governments displayed in the opening months of the crisis. It was an act of madness for a writer to try to document what was happening in real time while keeping up daily news reporting and guiding my small but brilliant Canberra news team, but I became obsessed with completing that mission. As David Marr notes of my methodology, I wanted to ask, *is all this decent?*, because I feared that politics being politics, and human nature being what it is, the collegiate spirit, that sense of common purpose demonstrated by our leaders, would peak and then subside. I wanted to capture and share what I witnessed as it happened, knowing that if I documented it later, the same history would be written through a different lens. I would ask different questions.

So, Australia has done well during COVID-19. Better than elsewhere. But most people I know have endured one of the worst years of their lives, and I wanted the essay to respect that sense of a society, of a political class, of an adviser class, being called to draw deeply on reserves. Hugh Mackay is, of course, correct to impose a sense of scale and historical perspective on what the country has experienced this year: COVID is not the Spanish flu, or a world war, and unemployment has not hit the depths of the Great Depression. But living with the virus has been hard, and as a society we are either considerably less tolerant of discomfort than our antecedents, or we have more means and opportunity to vent and agonise publicly about it.

Australians have trudged through winter, Victorians most of all. People have died. People have lost jobs and businesses they spent years nurturing. People have not seen loved ones for months because of closed borders. People who live alone have been isolated in their homes. Our shared sense of what's normal has shifted profoundly. I now flinch if I see people hugging with abandon on television – this feels like a reckless habit of a pre-pandemic age. Before I get into a lift at Parliament House during sitting weeks, I wonder if it's a good idea to seal myself in a confined space. I feel anxious at the thought of going to a cinema, which pre-pandemic was one of my great pleasures. There have been very few cases in Canberra for many months, but I still feel more comfortable at home than I do at a restaurant. I wonder how long I'll feel this way. If a vaccine turns up in the new year, if it works, if it can be rolled out before winter comes around again, will we all forget how this was? Will we revert to the mores of pre-pandemic life with the same delusions of invincibility that existed before COVID, or will we carry the plague with us? Is the coronavirus now etched in our collective consciousness? Will it, and the recession that has punctured Australia's remarkable three decades of growth, reshape not only our habits, but our collective sensibility?

Perhaps, adaptive and resilient species that we are, we can quickly unlearn the principal lesson of 2020: which was how to retreat. Perhaps the economy will rebound reasonably quickly because this is an artificial recession – a recession induced not by the cyclical booms and busts of capitalism or a credit crisis, but by governments for the purpose of saving lives. This one really was the recession we had to have – although no one was ever rash enough to characterise it in those Keating-esque terms. Perhaps, once governments bring us out of hibernation, we will all revert instantly and exuberantly to the habits of the consumer-driven convenience economy that existed, unchecked, unshadowed, until about the middle of March. Perhaps we will forget what we learnt over these months: that the convenience economy can only be enjoyed at times when the world is not staring down an existential threat. The pandemic also showed us the convenience economy is a function of globalisation, and it is an ecosystem of structural inequality that serves the whims and wants of people of means, with services delivered by an army of people with less rights, less protections and less opportunity than the rest of us – at least it will be, until automation removes even those prospects.

I wanted to document the opening of the crisis because what I witnessed was a succession of moral acts, and by moral acts I mean decisions that gave priority to saving lives. Dominic Kelly fears this insight – and my thesis that Morrison was largely pragmatic rather than ideological during the first wave – is the false narrative of unedifying insider journalism – a common critique of the work of the Canberra press gallery. I'm perfectly comfortable for Kelly to ask if I suffer from Stockholm syndrome, because that's a question I constantly ask myself. I don't, by the way. But I'm happy for readers to be the judge.

There is certainly a place for political analysis from a distance. But my task was to furnish a primary-source account of a crisis and a prime minister, and that requires proximity. I watched as days ebbed into nights, filling my notebooks with facts and quotes and transient observations. I remained at my desk, co-located with the decision-makers sequestered downstairs in the ministerial wing. Phil Coorey, political editor of *The Australian Financial Review*, who drifted in and out of my office seeking sugar and banter, was kind enough to review the essay. Phil spoke about trauma, and he's right. Some days the story was so huge we were completely overwhelmed. We rattled around the elegant empty spaces of Parliament House, pinging from briefings to press conferences, filing constantly. The wide circulation corridors of Romaldo Giurgola's magnificent building normally teem with spivs and staffers, but the only sound was our footfalls on the hardwood as we wore the pathways to and from the prime minister's courtyard and the committee rooms. When Australia went home for the lockdown, the people's house was funereal and pin-drop quiet, which was at first disconcerting, but then a salve for a reporter battling daily overload.

My colleagues and I watched and listened intently, reported exhaustively, and tried to respond to the public's hunger for factual information while at the same time managing our personal anxiety and intense fatigue so we could be reliable informants. It's true we managed those responsibilities better some days than others. I did not witness, nor render, perfection on the part of the government. I did not witness the end of ideology. I did not witness the end of self-interest, or venality, among Australia's political class – but I did watch and document a group of decision-makers valuing our common humanity, and trying not to fail.

Between the publication of the Quarterly Essay and me writing this response to the thoughtful and generous feedback the essay has generated, I've read Bob Woodward's terrific book *Rage*, which documents Donald Trump and the US administration's COVID-19 response. Much of Woodward's rendering of events felt very familiar to me, because leaders everywhere were facing the same threat, the same unknowns, the same weight of decision-making in the absence of perfect information. The Americans clearly knew a bit more about COVID earlier than we did in Australia, but the timeframes around the critical decision-making, and the inputs, were near identical. The main difference between America and Australia – apart from our political class accepting expert advice and Trump's dysfunctional White House veering between heeding advice and wild extemporisation – was the concentration span of the person in the top job.

If you've read my Quarterly Essay, you will know that I struggled to land a definitive portrait of my fleet-footed and shape-shifting subject, Australia's prime minister, Scott Morrison. I didn't use this particular analogy in the essay, but I've used it a number of times in sessions with readers as I reflected on the experience of writing a history in real time: our prime minister is like an outline in a colouring book. There's a bold black outline, a defined shape, but Morrison leaves you to choose your own colours to render him. He allows you to project what you need into his outline. This is a disconcerting quality for me, but it has been a successful strategy for him. In any case, I don't mention this to re-prosecute my Morrison character study, but to draw a comparison with Trump. Trump is fully hewn. There's no air gap. The American president is assertively present and fully fleshed out. He's so ubiquitous and oversized that the experience is repellent for all but the devotees. But what the Woodward history captures is a leader who can't concentrate at a time when concentration was absolutely necessary.

Our leaders, federal and state, concentrated during this crisis. They worked punishingly hard. They agonised in small groups, with experts floating in and out, trying to get the big calls right. I know this because I saw it. I saw their fear and their fatigue. I saw them running behind a crisis, trying to catch up and cushion the blows. Morrison wasn't distracted, and neither were the premiers. They were sometimes too slow, or wrong, or not quite sharp enough, or not in perfect lockstep, or they lacked the bandwidth to micromanage every element of every problem – but they weren't fundamentally impeded by their own narcissism. This sustained focus – combined with luck, with geography, with the fall of the seasons – explains why things have been better here than elsewhere, even though there was a second wave and there could be a third wave, as we are seeing now in the Northern Hemisphere as the winter closes in.

The sense of common purpose in the Australian political class spanned the middle of March through until about July, when the second wave in Victoria fractured the country's sense of pride and relief at initial success. The second wave heralded the return of partisanship. The Andrews government stumbled in managing the crisis – serious administrative missteps in contact tracing and in hotel quarantine – and went into damage control. The Commonwealth first distanced itself from the reversal, then turned on Andrews, intensifying the ferocity of its attacks to help mask its own failures in preparing aged-care homes for the crisis, failures the Morrison government continues to try to minimise. The country was treated to the perverse spectacle of Morrison agreeing that Victoria should be locked down, then punishing Andrews for following through. Senior Victorian ministers in Canberra carpet-bombed Andrews for his failures, then demanded the premier move faster with reopening, which was a peculiar kind of madness, because Andrews was never going to reopen the state before he felt the virus was contained.

Reopening too quickly would have put lives at risk, and also would have exposed Andrews to more bombardment from federal ministers. Andrews learnt that when things go bad, no one has your back. No one will stand with you in your hour of need. What the federal prosecution squad conveyed to the Victorian premier through their hectoring was: don't take any risks, because if you do, and disaster ensues, you are on your own. If Canberra wanted the state reopened, the most effective means of achieving that would have been to give Andrews some breathing space, some level of comfort that was a risk worth taking – but no comfort was forthcoming.

This reversion to politics as usual was all pretty depressing, because for a time things had been different. Not perfect. Just different. I'm not entirely certain how we unwind from the reversion to type, given Australia and the world is still mired in the crisis. That crisis still requires goodwill and cooperation to optimise its management. Rather than a government of nine, the federation now presents to the public as a resentful couple staying together for the sake of the children more than as a constructive partnership. But as Lesley Russell notes in her response, the findings of the essay, and the observations in this response, must be regarded as interim, because the long-term consequences of the virus are yet to be understood.

This was my first Quarterly Essay. I found it desperately hard, but the times are important, and I reported honestly, and shared what I saw. I hope the record stands the test of time. I was assisted in the project by many conversations, both on and off the record. Thank you for all the responses, which are beyond generous. I'm grateful to all the readers who have been in touch since publication with thoughts. This is a dialogue I cherish. Thank you to Chris Feik for improving both the thoughts and the words. I hope we work together again. Thank you also to Kirstie Innes-Will, who understood my voice and my objectives. The pandemic meant I was working with an editor and a copyeditor whom I'd never met, but their professionalism made it easy. I'm very grateful to Lenore Taylor, my friend and editor, and to my wonderful *Guardian Australia* Canberra team, who really didn't need me pursuing such an absorbing project at such a critical time but went on the journey with me with grace. Evie, Tom, Evan: I love you. Mark: I love you, and thank you. As usual, you went above and beyond.

Katharine Murphy

Phillip Coorey is political editor for *The Australian Financial Review*.

Elizabeth Flux's writing has been widely published, including in *The Saturday Paper*, *Guardian Australia*, *Island* and *Meanjin*.

Damien Freeman is the author of *Abbott's Right: The Conservative Tradition from Menzies to Abbott* and principal policy adviser at the PM Glynn Institute, the Australian Catholic University's public policy think-tank.

Dominic Kelly is an honorary research fellow at La Trobe University. He is the author of *Political Troglodytes and Economic Lunatics: The Hard Right in Australia*.

Celeste Liddle is an Arrernte woman living in Melbourne. She is a union organiser, social commentator and activist. Her writing has appeared in *Daily Life* (Fairfax), *Guardian Australia*, *New Matilda*, *Tracker Magazine* and *Eureka Street*.

Hugh Mackay is a social psychologist, researcher and author. His recent books include *Australia Reimagined* and *The Inner Self*.

David Marr is the author of *Patrick White: A Life*, *Panic*, *The High Price of Heaven* and *Dark Victory* (with Marian Wilkinson). He has written for *The Sydney Morning Herald*, *The Saturday Paper*, *Guardian Australia* and *The Monthly*, and been editor of the *National Times*, a reporter for *Four Corners* and presenter of ABC TV's *Media Watch*. He is the author of six bestselling Quarterly Essays.

Katharine Murphy has worked in Canberra's parliamentary press gallery since 1996 for *The Australian Financial Review*, *The Australian* and *The Age*, before joining *Guardian Australia*, where she is political editor. She won the Paul Lyneham Award for Excellence in Press Gallery Journalism in 2008 and has been a Walkley Award finalist twice. She is a director of the National Press Club and the author of *On Disruption*.

Lesley Russell is a non-resident fellow at the United States Studies Centre and an adjunct associate professor at the University of Sydney's Menzies Centre for Health Policy. She has worked as a senior policy adviser on health for the Democrats in the US House of Representatives, for the Obama administration and for the Australian Labor Party.

Laura Tingle is chief political correspondent for ABC TV's 7.30. She won the Paul Lyneham Award for Excellence in Press Gallery Journalism in 2004, and Walkley awards in 2005 and 2011. She is the author of *Chasing the Future: Recession, Recovery and the New Politics in Australia* and three previous acclaimed Quarterly Essays, *Great Expectations, Political Amnesia* and *Follow the Leader*.

James Walter is emeritus professor of politics at Monash University. His latest book is *The Pivot of Power: Australian Prime Ministers and Political Leadership, 1949–2016* (with Paul Strangio and Paul 't Hart).

Coming Soon

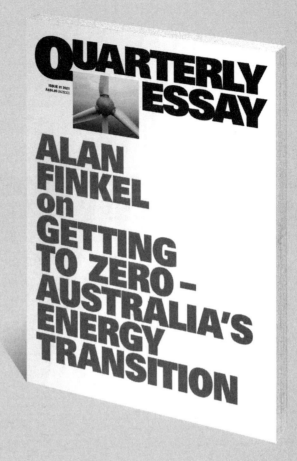

Quarterly Essay 81
Getting to Zero: Australia's
energy transition
Alan Finkel

The world is overheating, and despite good intentions and significant efforts, emissions increase nearly every year. The challenge is immense, but there are solutions.

In this lucid, persuasive essay, Australia's Chief Scientist, Alan Finkel, maps Australia's energy transition.

He focuses strongly on clean technologies, including the use of hydrogen, and addresses the challenge of intermittent supply. He shows how we can build a zero-emissions world.

Taking into account economics, science and emotions, *Getting to Zero* is an essential guide to how Australia can tackle the climate crisis with realism and ingenuity.

Out March 2021

WANT THE LATEST FROM QUARTERLY ESSAY?

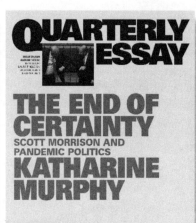

QUARTERLY ESSAY
BACK ISSUES

BACK ISSUES: (Prices include GST, postage and handling within Australia.) *Grey indicates out of stock.*

- [ ] **QE 1** ($17.99) Robert Manne *In Denial*
- [x] **QE 2** ($17.99) John Birmingham *Appeasing Jakarta*
- [x] **QE 3** ($17.99) Guy Rundle *The Opportunist*
- [x] **QE 4** ($17.99) Don Watson *Rabbit Syndrome*
- [ ] **QE 5** ($17.99) Mungo MacCallum *Girt By Sea*
- [x] **QE 6** ($17.99) John Button *Beyond Belief*
- [x] **QE 7** ($17.99) John Martinkus *Paradise Betrayed*
- [x] **QE 8** ($17.99) Amanda Lohrey *Groundswell*
- [x] **QE 9** ($17.99) Tim Flannery *Beautiful Lies*
- [x] **QE 10** ($17.99) Gideon Haigh *Bad Company*
- [ ] **QE 11** ($17.99) Germaine Greer *Whitefella Jump Up*
- [x] **QE 12** ($17.99) David Malouf *Made in England*
- [x] **QE 13** ($17.99) Robert Manne with David Corlett *Sending Them Home*
- [x] **QE 14** ($17.99) Paul McGeough *Mission Impossible*
- [x] **QE 15** ($17.99) Margaret Simons *Latham's World*
- [x] **QE 16** ($17.99) Raimond Gaita *Breach of Trust*
- [x] **QE 17** ($17.99) John Hirst *'Kangaroo Court'*
- [x] **QE 18** ($17.99) Gail Bell *The Worried Well*
- [x] **QE 19** ($17.99) Judith Brett *Relaxed & Comfortable*
- [x] **QE 20** ($17.99) John Birmingham *A Time for War*
- [x] **QE 21** ($17.99) Clive Hamilton *What's Left?*
- [x] **QE 22** ($17.99) Amanda Lohrey *Voting for Jesus*
- [ ] **QE 23** ($17.99) Inga Clendinnen *The History Question*
- [ ] **QE 24** ($17.99) Robyn Davidson *No Fixed Address*
- [x] **QE 25** ($17.99) Peter Hartcher *Bipolar Nation*
- [x] **QE 26** ($17.99) David Marr *His Master's Voice*
- [x] **QE 27** ($17.99) Ian Lowe *Reaction Time*
- [x] **QE 28** ($17.99) Judith Brett *Exit Right*
- [ ] **QE 29** ($17.99) Anne Manne *Love & Money*
- [x] **QE 30** ($17.99) Paul Toohey *Last Drinks*
- [ ] **QE 31** ($17.99) Tim Flannery *Now or Never*
- [x] **QE 32** ($17.99) Kate Jennings *American Revolution*
- [x] **QE 33** ($17.99) Guy Pearse *Quarry Vision*
- [ ] **QE 34** ($17.99) Annabel Crabb *Stop at Nothing*
- [ ] **QE 35** ($17.99) Noel Pearson *Radical Hope*
- [x] **QE 36** ($17.99) Mungo MacCallum *Australian Story*
- [ ] **QE 37** ($17.99) Waleed Aly *What's Right?*
- [x] **QE 38** ($17.99) David Marr *Power Trip*
- [x] **QE 39** ($17.99) Hugh White *Power Shift*

- [x] **QE 40** ($17.99) George Megalogenis *Trivial Pursuit*
- [x] **QE 41** ($17.99) David Malouf *The Happy Life*
- [x] **QE 42** ($17.99) Judith Brett *Fair Share*
- [x] **QE 43** ($17.99) Robert Manne *Bad News*
- [x] **QE 44** ($17.99) Andrew Charlton *Man-Made World*
- [x] **QE 45** ($17.99) Anna Krien *Us and Them*
- [ ] **QE 46** ($17.99) Laura Tingle *Great Expectations*
- [x] **QE 47** ($17.99) David Marr *Political Animal*
- [x] **QE 48** ($17.99) Tim Flannery *After the Future*
- [x] **QE 49** ($17.99) Mark Latham *Not Dead Yet*
- [x] **QE 50** ($17.99) Anna Goldsworthy *Unfinished Business*
- [ ] **QE 51** ($17.99) David Marr *The Prince*
- [x] **QE 52** ($17.99) Linda Jaivin *Found in Translation*
- [x] **QE 53** ($17.99) Paul Toohey *That Sinking Feeling*
- [x] **QE 54** ($17.99) Andrew Charlton *Dragon's Tail*
- [ ] **QE 55** ($17.99) Noel Pearson *A Rightful Place*
- [x] **QE 56** ($17.99) Guy Rundle *Clivosaurus*
- [x] **QE 57** ($17.99) Karen Hitchcock *Dear Life*
- [x] **QE 58** ($17.99) David Kilcullen *Blood Year*
- [x] **QE 59** ($17.99) David Marr *Faction Man*
- [ ] **QE 60** ($17.99) Laura Tingle *Political Amnesia*
- [x] **QE 61** ($17.99) George Megalogenis *Balancing Act*
- [x] **QE 62** ($17.99) James Brown *Firing Line*
- [ ] **QE 63** ($17.99) Don Watson *Enemy Within*
- [ ] **QE 64** ($17.99) Stan Grant *The Australian Dream*
- [x] **QE 65** ($17.99) David Marr *The White Queen*
- [x] **QE 66** ($17.99) Anna Krien *The Long Goodbye*
- [x] **QE 67** ($17.99) Benjamin Law *Moral Panic 101*
- [x] **QE 68** ($17.99) Hugh White *Without America*
- [x] **QE 69** ($17.99) Mark McKenna *Moment of Truth*
- [x] **QE 70** ($17.99) Richard Denniss *Dead Right*
- [x] **QE 71** ($17.99) Laura Tingle *Follow the Leader*
- [x] **QE 72** ($17.99) Sebastian Smee *Net Loss*
- [x] **QE 73** ($17.99) Rebecca Huntley *Australia Fair*
- [x] **QE 74** ($17.99) Erik Jensen *The Prosperity Gospel*
- [x] **QE 75** ($17.99) Annabel Crabb *Men at Work*
- [x] **QE 76** ($17.99) Peter Hartcher *Red Flag*
- [x] **QE 77** ($24.99) Margaret Simons *Cry Me a River*
- [x] **QE 78** ($24.99) Judith Brett *The Coal Curse*
- [x] **QE 79** ($24.99) Katharine Murphy *The End of Certainty*

Please include this form with delivery and payment details overleaf.
Back issues also available as eBooks at **quarterlyessay.com**

SUBSCRIBE TO RECEIVE
10% OFF THE COVER PRICE

☐ **ONE-YEAR PRINT AND DIGITAL SUBSCRIPTION: $89.99**

- Print edition × 4
- Home delivery
- Full digital access to all past issues, including downloadable eBook files
- Access iPad & iPhone app
- Access Android app

☐ **TICK HERE TO COMMENCE SUBSCRIPTION WITH THE CURRENT ISSUE**

DELIVERY AND PAYMENT DETAILS

DELIVERY DETAILS:

NAME:

ADDRESS:

EMAIL: PHONE:

PAYMENT DETAILS: Enclose a cheque/money order made out to Schwartz Books Pty Ltd.
Or debit my credit card (MasterCard, Visa and Amex accepted).
Freepost: Quarterly Essay, Reply Paid 90094, Carlton VIC 3053
All prices include GST, postage and handling.

CARD NO.

EXPIRY DATE: /   CCV: AMOUNT: $

PURCHASER'S NAME: SIGNATURE:

Subscribe online at **quarterlyessay.com/subscribe** • Freecall: 1800 077 514 • Phone: 03 9486 0288
Email: subscribe@quarterlyessay.com (please do not send electronic scans of this form)